May peace be with you,

Alice J Miller

voiceoftheturtledove.com

Finding Peace In Our Thyme

A Psychotherapist's Path

Alice G. Miller, PhD

Photography by Roy Sewall

Copyright © 2017 Alice G. Miller, PhD
All rights reserved.

ISBN-10: 1541220870
ISBN-13: 9781541220874

Dedicated to the Memory of

Reverend Rodney Shaw

who so deeply

believed in

and lived

in peace…..

…….and

touched my heart.

Contents

One	Once Again Eden	1
Two	A Thyme for Peace	7
Three	Giving Peace a Chance	13
Four	Be Here Now	21
Five	Be There Now	25
Six	Square Brown Rooms	35
Seven	Finding Peace for the Spider Woman	49
Eight	An Instrument of Peace	61
Nine	Celebrate Life	71
Ten	A Scorpion in Eden	83
Eleven	God's Broken Children	91
Twelve	Us and Them	103
Thirteen	A Thyme to Heal	111
Fourteen	Love is a Verb	141
Fifteen	No Big Deal	151
Sixteen	Growing Up in Eden	157
Seventeen	The Web of Life	165
Eighteen	Breathing Room	173
Nineteen	Waging Peace	181
Twenty	The Voice of the Turtle Dove	193

Introduction

The road to peace, like the "Road to Hell," is paved with good intentions.

World peace, I fear, is still not going to happen until peoples' hearts begin to change. And I am still working on mine.

Learning to accept and to love openly are lessons that I have learned from good teachers who have touched my life along the way.

It was my grandmother, Bobby, who first showed me, by example, that beyond love for family, there can also be caring for the world and for others, even when they look, talk and think differently than we do. And that was just the beginning.

For me, the path to peace has been a long and winding one. And that path goes right through the garden. As a gardener I have found a sacred space for spiritual renewal in my own life. There is a sense of peace and meditation in the daily task of planting and nurturing a place of beauty and a habitat for wildlife.

As the garden blooms with my creativity –and nature's—it also opens a new door for peace in my life. I cannot write about one without the other. So, this is a book written both for gardeners and for seekers of peace.

I have yet to solve the dilemma of world peace, but I do believe that it starts with inner peace. And I know something about that.

Elie Wiesel would understand those feelings. Mr. Wiesel, a survivor of the Holocaust, has written many haunting stories of the Jewish people who survived, but will never forget the suffering of the Holocaust years.

His stories have a universal theme of the "lost," telling their story and finding their own path and their own relationship to God and to community with each other. Wiesel tells this tale in different words in his story "The Gates of the Forest." His is the traditional telling of this old tale of the Rabbi's prayers to God.

The great rabbi Baal Shem-Tov loved his people. Whenever he sensed they were in danger, he would go to a secret place in the woods, light a special fire, and say a special prayer. Then, without fail, his people would be saved from danger.

Baal Shem-Tov passed on and his disciple, Magrid of Mezritch, came to lead the people. Whenever he sensed his people were in danger, he would go to the secret place in the woods. "Dear God," he would say, "I don't know how to light the special fire, but I know the special prayer. Please let that be good enough." It was, and the people would once again be saved from danger.

When Magrid passed on, he was succeeded by another rabbi, the Rabbi Moshe-leib of Sasov, and whenever he heard that his people were in danger, he would go to the secret place in the woods. "Dear God," he would say. "I don't know how to make the special fire, I don't know how to say the special prayer, but I know this secret place in the woods. Please let that be good enough." It was, and the people would again be saved from danger.

When Rabbi Moshe passed, he was succeeded by Rabbi Israel of Rozhyn, and whenever somebody told him that his people were in danger, he didn't even get out of his armchair. He could only bow his head and shrug his shoulders. "Dear God," he would pray, "I don't even know the secret place in the woods All I know is the story, and I'm hoping that's good enough." It was and his people would be saved.

God made people because he loves stories. One can only hope that God does love a good story. For that is what this book is about – the story of a pilgrimage. If that is, you define a pilgrimage as a long journey or a search of deep moral or spiritual significance.

Then this is a story of the pilgrimage of an unknown, unremarkable woman, who never did any of the "big" things in life. But that's okay. Sometimes God is in the "little" stuff. So, maybe this book is for all the other "little" people.

We are all pilgrims, telling and re-telling our story, one way or another. As a psychotherapist I have walked with other people as they tell their story and struggle with making changes in their own lives.

Good therapy is not about changing other people. It is only about being a catalyst for whatever changes they choose to make. as they grow into the person they feel that they were meant to be.

This is why I refer to the people I see as "clients" rather than as "patients." For my clients, this is not a "sick-well" model. It is a change model, which reflects what has sometimes been called the Social Work Life Model of Practice.

Therapeutically speaking, I have begun to speak of evolving, rather than changing. The word "change" can carry the implication that you are not okay now, but that with "change" you will become okay. To evolve gives the message that you are already okay, but you are now becoming even better.

Reverend Rodney Shaw gave me that message many years ago when we were both members of a small, social concerns group. At the time I did not realize that as a minister, pacifist and author, he was a major force in the peace movement. To me, he was just Rodney.

Although I rarely agreed with his belief system, occasionally, I thought it was funny to quote the views of my father who, politically, was slightly to the right of Attila the Hun. At the time, I found it amusing to make irreverent suggestions, like resolving the Viet Nam "conflict" with a few twenty megaton bombs, while others in the group prayed for peace.

Rodney never tried to change me. He just smiled, expressed some kinder methods of problem resolution and continued to care about me, just as I was. And, funny thing, I began to want to be a little more like Rodney.

Being with Rodney always felt like you were just walking together with his arm around your shoulder. And that's just how Rodney was. He didn't lead you. He just walked beside you. And that, I believe, is where peace begins.

Walking together.

I am still on the road to becoming a pacifist. It remains a work in progress. As evidenced in later chapters, this is far from being a straight path. Sometimes life just happens and everything I learned from Rodney goes straight out the window.

As Mary, my more peace-evolved sister-in-law likes to point out: "Alice, you can't call yourself a pacifist and go around kicking people in the groin just because they threaten you." Actually, you can. And besides, it only happened once.

Sometimes we just have to reconcile ourselves with our life experiences. I am still working on that. And the garden helps. When life intrudes it is the garden that brings me back to my spiritual journey. It is the garden that keeps me on the path. It would be hard to imagine being so at one with the earth and not believing in God.

I may not be sufficiently enlightened to say that I "know" God. That always sounds so grandiose. But, even if I don't "know" Him. I am certainly aware of Him.

And, since God loves a good story, that is what this book is about; sharing my pilgrimage on the road to peace—with a little help from my garden – and my friends.

one

Once Again Eden

The Lord God planted a garden
in the first white days of the world,
and set there an Angel Warden,
in a garment of light unfurled.
So near to the peace of heaven,
that the hawk might nest with the wren,
for there in the cool of the even',
God walked with the first of men.
The kiss of the sun for pardon,
The song of the birds for mirth,
one is nearer God's heart in a garden
than anywhere else on earth.
—Dorothy Frances Gurney

Once Again Eden

"Earth Woman" was the *non de plum* I once used for a column, which I occasionally wrote for a church newsletter. Very few people actually read the column. Nonetheless, those articles actually puffed me up, even if one reader did comment that most of my writing made me sound like some "nerdy, little tree hugger."

Well, so was Al Gore and *he* won the Nobel Peace Prize. So, I guess that puts me in good company. Although in my case, writing about "Earth Woman" was never about scholarship. It was about the creation of the garden as a spiritual place, a place where peace begins.

Creating this spiritual place has been a 25-plus years of labor of love. The lush woodland of today was once only a barren acre dotted with a few scraggly apple trees. But, we fell in love with a fantasy garden. So we bought the house and built the woods.

Now those years of labor have transformed that bare acre into a secluded woodland sanctuary with giant evergreens, winding paths, ponds and sunny patches of ever-changing blooms. And we did it all ourselves. Lest there be any doubt of that, I still have the banged up back to show for it.

It's been said that for all the hours that the gardener spends digging, bending, pulling and lifting, God should have thought to provide a stainless steel spine, complete with a hinge. That didn't happen.

Nonetheless, it has been worth every muscle-straining, bone-crunching, spinal disc re-aligning moment. Those little things are just the physical part. The joyful part has been creating a beautiful, sun dappled woodland with food and shelter for birds, butterflies, frogs, turtles, chipmunks, rabbits, toads, raccoons and an occasional fox.

It is Eden.

The Garden of Eden is an age-old metaphor for peace on earth. That very earth as we know it, but just a little closer to the peaceful earth that once was. I believe that it is through the nurturing experience of being in that peaceful place that we become more able to fulfill the goal of Tikkun Olam, as it is expressed in the Talmud. That responsibility encompasses the repair of the world; whether it is through social justice, healing the brokenness in humanity, or repairing the earth itself.

For me, creating that Eden has been a long, circuitous route. The journey itself has been a source of peace in my life. The poet, Emily Dickinson, expressed this experience so simply when she wrote of creating a prairie:

> *To make a prairie it takes a clover and one bee.*
> *One clover and a bee,*
> *And revery.*
> *The revery alone will do,*
> *If bees are few.*

For the gardener, it is in that experience of revery when we connect with the earth and touch the spiritual within ourselves that, for a moment or more, we can know peace.

Emily Dickinson's prairie, the prairie of our ancestors, now remains primarily in the pages of our history books. Thousands and thousands of acres that were once covered with lush, green grasses and a multitude of plants are now covered with cement.

They have been replaced with office buildings, shopping centers and parking lots. Many of the plants, animals and insects that once filled the prairies now continue to lose their habitats and will follow the remnants of the prairies into extinction.

So, the creation of a garden, however large or small, can become a gift of habitat back to the earth; not to mention, a gift to ourselves; a quiet refuge where we can experience the healing power of nature.

I believe that, ever since Eden, we were meant to return to a green place; not to be living a life filled only with city streets, cramped, artificially lit office cubicles and daily doses of job-related high alerts. There is a physical cost to be paid for all of this pressure. That price is announced with tension, stress, headaches, anxiety and depression.

Finding relief from all this stress can be a lot closer than your neighborhood pharmacy. Just a long walk through tree-lined back streets, abandoning your cares and letting your mind focus on the grassy lawns, flowering shrubs and plants; or allowing yourself to be relaxed and enveloped in the soft green of a quiet garden.

Works for me. The cares of the world recede when I am immersed in the garden. Here I can let go of all my anger toward: terrorists, narcissistic, self-serving politicians, war mongers, racists, child abusers, frackers and all the assorted destroyers of the earth.

That healing allows me to keep my heart open to all that is good and beautiful in the world and to continue to live my life with compassion.

Compassion, that feeling of empathy for another, is usually coupled with a strong desire to help people reduce the pain in their lives. Sometimes the feelings of empathy engendered by walking with a client, who is going through extreme trauma and pain, can leave a psychotherapist physically and emotionally exhausted.

As a therapist, I value the gift that allows me to walk with a client through their difficult journey. But, I have learned that I not only need to walk with my client *in* through that pain, but also, for myself, to later walk *out*. And, for me, that walk has always been right through the garden gate.

Throughout the week, my woodland retreat is, for me, a sacred space. Whenever possible, I start my day in the garden. On warm days, I like to sit cross-legged on the old lumpy rock at the edge of the pond; listening to the waterfall bubbling and watching the fish darting about waiting for their snack.

Although some days there are no fish to dart about because the raccoons have sneaked in the night before and treated themselves to some tasty hors d'oeuvres. This is just a price you have to pay for habitat. There will always be somebody munching on somebody else. I've finally gotten used to it. Besides, the birds, rabbits, squirrels, turtles and chipmunks more than make up for the bad attitude of the raccoons.

This garden has been designed to provide habitat for all these creatures and even the occasional red fox. So, in addition to the evergreen pines, spruce and holly and the underbrush for shelter, there is an abundance of viburnum, nandina and dogwood. The birds will never lack for a ready supply of summer and winter snacks.

And for the pleasure of the two-legged creatures, the garden contains a series of garden rooms, each connected to the other by a winding path of pine needle mulch.

The paths meander through the meditation garden, into the butterfly garden, through the "children's park" and down a long, winding raccoon path.

The many paths are all narrow, not wide, because this is not a place designed for speed; it is a place for meditation, a place to walk slowly. This is an experience to savor and to renew our biological connection to the earth. It is a place to feel the presence of the divine through nature.

For this is Eden.

Recently, a visiting friend, who arrived feeling stressed and tired, decided that first she would like to walk through the woodland and *then* spend some time together. So, I lounged in the sunroom and read the paper while she walked.

When my friend reappeared it was to report that, once again, the garden had worked its magic. I was not surprised. For, as the inscription carved over the arched entryway to the meditation garden reads: *Peace To All Who Enter.*

two

A Thyme for Peace

Blessed are the peacemakers
For they shall be called
The Children of God.
—Matthew 5 – 9

A Thyme for Peace

The garden's message, "Peace to All Who Enter," is only the beginning. "Pass it on" is the next step. When you re-enter the world from a peaceful place, it impacts how you experience your own life. Now you are able to view others with more compassion and less impatience.

Sometimes it is also the experience of "community" with the fellowship of caring and mutually supportive friends that makes this experience possible.

Early in my life it was my good fortune to share in just this sort of fellowship with a small Christian social concerns group that began in a local church.

The "concern group" continued for several years, even after individual members moved on to join other churches where they could participate in more local and world mission activities. It was in the concern group that I first met Reverend Rodney Shaw, who started me on the road to pacifism, a pilgrimage I have yet to complete.

The group came at just the right time in my life. An earlier church experience had left me disillusioned with the seeming lack of concern within the church for anyone other than themselves.

In retrospect, I now realize that sometimes an individual church can stray from the ideals of the church universal. All too often, that condition is a reflection of the leadership. Ralph Waldo Emerson could have been speaking of the church when he wrote, "an institution is the lengthened shadow of one man." And it is my opinion that the pastor of that particular church cast a very puny shadow indeed.

I imagine that the pastor assumed that by taking the stance of a powerful man "in charge," everyone would be awed by his strength.

His need to control was awesome. He said little in the pulpit, but spent considerable time and volume saying it.

What a contrasting experience the concern group and Rodney Shaw proved to be. There, people shared their beliefs and actually listened to each other. Rodney Shaw inspired us all with his belief that peace begins in the hearts of people, who then touch other people.

The concern group reflected that belief in the caring and concern that they felt for each other and for the world. At the time, my concerns tended toward local, not global, issues. I was the exact opposite of Charles Schultz's Charlie Brown, whose famous social opinion was: "I love mankind. It's people I can't stand." I, on the other hand, loved people, but found it difficult to feel for mankind, who I experienced as vague, distant and somewhat annoying.

As a younger member of the group, I suspect that I may have behaved in much the same way that I did as the younger child in my family of origin. My older brother, Dana, typical of the eldest child in many families, was responsible, earnest and reliable. I, on the other hand, was called the "willow-the-wisp."

"You would get in a lot less trouble if you acted more like your brother," was the litany I grew up with. All too often, I found it more fun to be a smart aleck instead. So it is not surprising that in the concern group I frequently enjoyed a good laugh, even when others were deeply pondering over major social issues.

But, little by little, I was also learning how an individual can, on a human level, foster the conditions for peace. Rodney exemplified this by word and deed. Sometimes this meant that he was not above an occasional bit of genteel arm-twisting in the cause of civil and human rights.

One of his daughters recalls that Rodney always had to go the second mile. It was not enough for him to simply participate as one of the 22 whites on the historic 54-mile Selma, Alabama march for civil rights. Afterwards he mobilized clergy members nationwide to battle racist attacks on the march and took on the Selma mayor in a David Susskind TV debate.

"Don't you think the ministers had better get out of the political and social revolution and get back to saving souls?" the mayor queried Rodney. "Would Jesus advocate civil disobedience?"

Rodney replied, "I don't think that Jesus was crucified for obeying the law."

And that was Rodney.

***

In the early days of the concern group I was scarcely aware of the profound impact those evenings were having on my life. Eventually, I realized how deeply inspired I was by the actions of Rodney Shaw and by his level of caring for each of us. It was Rodney who motivated my early steps on the road to peace. Of course, it was some of those steps that led to being gassed at the Justice Department. But that is another story.

I have often wondered if Rodney ever realized how much he had touched the direction of my life. Probably not. I doubt that anyone ever realizes how much he or she may have impacted the life of another person. But, as we are reminded in the Talmud:

> *He that gives*
> *should not remember.*
> *He that receives*
> *should never forget.*

I will always remember. I think that a perfect metaphor for that experience can be found in an anonymous, untitled poem found taped on the wall of a youth services center more than thirty years ago. No one knew how it got there, or who wrote it. But it spoke to me then, and now it hangs on my wall.

> *Ever feel like a frog?*
> *Slow....low....ugly....drooped....pooped.*
> *The frog feeling comes when you*
> *want to be bright, but feel dull,*
> *want to share, but feel selfish,*
> *want to be thankful, but feel resentment,*
> *want to be big, but feel small,*
> *want to care, but are indifferent.*

Each of us has found himself on a lily pad on the
great river of life…frightened and disgusted…….
Too froggish to budge.

We all know the story of the frog.
But he wasn't really a frog…..he was a prince
who looked and felt like a frog.
Only the kiss of a beautiful maiden could save him.
But since when do people kiss frogs?
At any rate, it happened and the frog experienced
a great reversal….a metamorphosis,
a transformation, a change
from something UGLY
into SOMEONE beautiful.

That's what God does for people.
He takes us where we are
and works changes in us so there is
an alteration in structure,
in constitution, in appearance.

We become new persons
And miracle of miracles,
He can touch and transform other lives
through us.
God changes frogs into princes.
So what are we about?
Kissing frogs.
What else?

Although Rodney was a leader on the Methodist Board of Social Concerns in civil and human rights movements, world peace and population control; and a mover and a shaker, implementing legislation on the national scene—to me, he will always be Rodney —"kisser of frogs."

three

Giving Peace a Chance

*War and peace start in the hearts
of individuals. Strangely enough,
even though all beings would like
to live in peace, our method for
obtaining peace over the generations
seems not to be very effective. We seek
peace and happiness by going to war.*
—Pema Chodron, Buddhist nun

Giving Peace a Chance

Just as there has always been a garden in my life, there has always been a place to retreat and find peace; a mountain- top of sorts.

But, sometimes in life it isn't enough to just breathe in the earth and feel gratitude. Sometimes you have to leave the mountaintop and be in the world in whatever way you may feel called. And that is exactly how I once felt about Viet Nam.

In recent years I have watched in horror as the Middle East, America's current Viet Nam, explodes, shattering more lives and other countries.

For me, Viet Nam was the wake-up call. In those early days, as a new, young wife, I still spouted some of my parents' political views, which were slightly to the right of Attila the Hun. But, as I became more involved with the church concerns group, I began to understand the cost of war in human lives.

Gradually, the influence of my peace-pedaling mentors began to rub off. At the time, I was just a very young, naïve suburban girl playing with my new little wife role. I had never dreamed of picketing Dow Chemical or marching on the White House.

And yet, one cold November Saturday, amidst clouds of tear gas, I found myself linking arms with the other marshals of the New Mobe Peace Demonstration to form a human buffer between the peace lines and a mob of angry, extremist rioters.

This sort of involvement had never been in my plans. But, witnessing a somber March Against Death the previous Friday night had so moved me that I was drawn to march for peace on Saturday.

When I looked at the endless death procession representing such a huge sacrifice of human lives, I was no longer willing, or able, to be a part of the silent majority. I wanted to join the other thousands, who felt the same way—to walk with them and say, "I care, too."

Somehow, that Saturday, as the day wore on and tensions increased, I ended up as a newly minted and totally untrained peace marshal. Wearing a pale blue armband that identified me as a peacekeeper, I stood on Constitution Avenue in Washington, D.C. and thrilled to watch as a quarter of a million people filed by.

There were banners and flags and sandals and bell bottoms and baby strollers and bears and boots and business suits and capes and headbands and veterans uniforms and costumed crazies and grandmothers in support stockings.

This was America marching by.

The "vibes" were great. These people had come together, not just as separate cultural, religious, social or ethnic groups, but as human beings joined in a common bond to protest the killing of their brothers and sisters. It was togetherness. And we all knew that we were a part of something very big.

Meanwhile, the nation's president, who so recently had urged us all to move forward together in unity, elected to watch the football game while a quarter of a million people tried to tell him something.

There were Quakers with placards saying, "There are no winners in a war, only survivors." And a pacifist asking, "How many more must die before we give peace a chance?"

A Jewish couple carried a sign saying, "Hitler was supported by the silent majority." Other signs bore the grim reminder, "The 40,000 war dead *are* the silent majority."

"Viet Nam —Love it or leave it," suggested some ex-GIs. Others were more militant, chanting "Hell No, we won't go." There were silent coffin bearers and a man pulling a large wooden cross. Individuals all had their say.

"Here is one Boston attorney who is over 40 and for peace," read one placard. A sprightly matron proudly proclaimed, "This Effete Grandmother is for peace." And the mothers came in droves. "Not Our Sons. Not Their Sons," protested the signs.

But, like the snake in Eden, there were also the destructive militants. The crazies, the Yippies and the Weathermen came in full costume to air their more radical views. They were but a small minority who were tolerated in brotherhood, but not supported.

"Ho Ho Ho Chi Minh," chanted the marching Yippies. But they were drowned out by the New Mobe Marshals, who quickly flanked them while singing the theme song of the day, "All we are saying is give peace a chance."

"Revolution!" bellowed the crazies as they marched down the street.

"No! Peace!" a marshal yelled back.

"Revolution, then Peace!" roared the crazies at the top of their lungs.

"Peace and then more Peace" returned the marshals. The people on the sidelines took it from there. "Peace Now. Peace Now. Peace Now." they shouted.

Part of the credit for the success of this great demonstration went to the Metropolitan Police, who kept their cool the entire time. Despite being cold and fatigued from working overtime and under the constant strain of such a tremendous responsibility with a quarter of a million people in the streets, they were polite, friendly and extremely efficient.

Whenever possible, the police let the marshals handle the crowd. And it worked, because the crowd wanted it to work. To keep the marchers on the designated route, the marshals often had to link arms and hold a line.

I am not kidding myself about my own role as a marshal. When you weigh in at 105 pounds you really don't have much clout. Most of the men in that crowd could have easily tossed me aside. Yet, when I yelled, "Don't break the line," the vast majority of people in that crowd cooperated willingly. There was a feeling of shared responsibility to make this, one of the biggest and greatest demonstrations, come off peacefully. And that is what held the line.

The sense of oneness of purpose gave us all a feeling of community with each other. This was especially true among the marshals. We were all cold and hungry, so everyone shared whatever they had.

"Here, have a bite of my apple," said the man next to me. The apple looked well bitten already. Soon a tuna sandwich came by.

"Eat some and pass it on," I was told. A teacher from Philadelphia decided that I looked hungry and fished in the bottom of his backpack for a bologna sandwich that he had been saving for dinner.

Occasionally, someone would come by with a cup of hot coffee and pass it through the crowd. Joining together for that sandwich and that coffee was a time of oneness. We were all feeling like a part of something bigger. It was not unlike being in church and breaking bread together.

Sometimes, in the Presbyterian Church, the communion bread and wine are passed from one person to another, as each "serves" the person next to them. That Saturday with the peace marchers felt just like that. It was communion.

We were total strangers, yet it was as though, in this spirit of community, we were somehow all connected, one with the other. I think we all realized that this was what the peace march was all about— the way people were meant to be with each other.

Sadly, there was a small group of militants who did not share those feelings. Except for the degree of violence, it was not unlike those times in later years when the Green Peace protestors, who supported the noble cause of saving the earth, then spoiled it with great displays of anger. And that is exactly what happened the day of the New Mobe March, when the voices of anger tried to drown out the voices of peace.

After the march was almost over and the crowds had dwindled, several hundred wild-eyed Yippies and SDS radicals, joined by heavy crowds of onlookers, stormed the Justice Department. Shouting obscenities, they demanded the release of Bobby Seale and the Chicago Eight.

Those of us marshals who were still wearing our blue armbands and also happened to be in the vicinity of the Justice Department, were urgently summoned to the side of the building.

It was the hope of the leaders that our remaining small group of marshals could hold off a violent confrontation between the police and the rioters, before the crazies could tarnish the impact of an otherwise powerful and peaceful demonstration.

Linking arms, we marshals formed a tight block between the police line and the SDS mob. Now the rioters began calling *us* the "pigs," throwing rocks and smashing windows.

Many people in the mob ripped the signs off the planks they had been carrying, which were now converted into clubs. It was both pitiful and terrifying to see the looks of hatred on the faces of this group, so bent on creating destruction in the name of peace.

By this time the police were in tight formation with their helmets on and their own clubs ready. And there we were—a scraggly line of marshals, terrified but arms still linked, sandwiched between a line of heavily armed police, and another line of the out-of-control, club wielding, rock throwing rioters.

When the rocks began to fly, I suddenly realized that when it comes to a real confrontation and the risk of serious bodily injury, I am not the powerful person I thought I was. At that moment all I wanted to do was to run as fast and as far as possible. Let someone else give peace a chance.

But running away was not an option. The marshals were frantically calling to "Hold the line!" So none of us felt that we could just break the line and leave the other marshals with even less support.

There were screamed curses and the sounds of glass breaking all around us. Patience exhausted, the police whipped on their gas masks. Then the rioters, who clearly had come prepared, started putting on *their* gas masks, too. Now the fear was rapidly spreading among the marshals. We were trapped and terrified.

As the first police gas canister exploded, the student next to me showed me how to pull the collar of my turtleneck sweater up over my face. This gave me some protection, but it was not enough. Being gassed is a profoundly miserable and painful experience. The tear gas felt like it was burning up my eyes and seeping into every pore of my body.

"I'm choking to death!" I screamed in panic. The nausea and the gasping struggle for air was even worse than the pain.

"Marshals, clear the area!" roared the police as they raced forward with batons swinging wildly. The peace marshals, who had now become a hindrance to riot control, were slung out of the way so the officers could plow into the rioting mob. Pure bedlam ensued with people screaming and running in all directions. Blindly, I kept running, all the while, knowing that if I fell I would be trampled. It was the final straw.

"One side is throwing rocks at me and the other side is gassing and slugging me," I sobbed. "What am I doing here?" But, I knew what I was doing there and it mattered. A bit of shoving by the police was a small price to pay for knowing that now the riot would finally be squelched. And I had a new- found respect for the cops, who daily put themselves at risk to protect the rest of us.

What is really sad is that later, on the basis of the irresponsible action of this small minority, a lunatic fringe, the Attorney General, no paragon of virtue himself, publicly condemned the sincere protest of a quarter of a million people.

Had he actually been at the Justice Department that afternoon, the Attorney General would have come closer to understanding the real spirit of the New Mobe. He would have seen the actions of another minority group, a small band of marshals, who stood in the window wells of the Justice Department and pleaded with the angry mob not to destroy the peace demonstration with violence.

They remained in a shower of rocks and shattering glass with their arms outstretched in the peace sign. They were there because they thought that it was worth taking a few risks for the cause of peace. I think they were right.

And that is why I marched.

four

Be Here Now

We can never obtain peace
in the outer world until
we make peace with ourselves.
—Dalai Lama

Be Here Now

Marching and speaking for peace is always a good thing. But first, it helps to experience peace from within. To "be here now" is about experiencing that peace and that, for me, is what mindfulness is all about.

There is no mystical mumbo-jumbo involved. Mindfulness just means being intensely aware of the present moment. Not yesterday, which has already passed, or tomorrow, which has yet to come. But today, right now, in this moment.

In mindfulness there is an intense awareness of, not an escape from, reality. That means accepting that reality, whether it is joy or sadness, loving or anger, and learning to observe those feelings without judging. Then, with a heightened awareness, you are free to offer up those feelings.

When it comes to letting go of negativity, I have found the garden to be a good teacher. But that experience is not about to happen if I stride down the path thinking only about today's hurts or tomorrow's projects. For then, I will never truly have been in the garden.

It is only when I feel a oneness with the force of all that living beauty, that I am free to let go of angers and resentments and experience the calm that Thich Nhat Hahn calls "being peace."

These mindful moments have been transforming experiences in my life. Finding this space of peace became my safe harbor in the storm and furor of the 2016 Presidential elections. I would like to say that achieving this level of awareness has completely changed my life. It has powerfully changed my life but, not completely. Not yet.

Never was this more obvious than the afternoon I braved the crowds at the local shopping center during the pre-Christmas madhouse.

Tired, cold and battling a fierce sinus headache, I stood on the curb waiting for a ride.

Behind me a stalwart Salvation Army volunteer rang her brass bell, jangling every frazzled nerve in my head. When no donations were dropped in her little tin bucket, this sturdy soldier of Christ began to ring her bell still harder and harder.

Mindfulness went right out the window as I fantasized shouting, "Will you stop that dam ringing!" while I throttled her with the ribbons of her little Christian Army bonnet.

Like I have said, I have a long way to go.

So, at times like this, when I feel a need to return to my kinder, gentler self and, to once again become calm and reflective, it is the garden that provides that sanctuary.

Never is that peace more profound then on those rare mornings when I arise early and enter the world of the garden as it awakens.

Sitting cross-legged on my prayer rock, the big, lumpy old stone at the edge of the pond, it is time to take slow, deep breaths and inhale the essence of the garden. I can only begin to describe the experience of heightened awareness that follows; a kaleidoscope of all my senses.

> *I sit on my prayer rock and I see....*
> *The garden lying in silence,*
> *waiting for me;*
>
> *the tall, arching ferns,*
> *still frosty with cobwebs;*
> *the pond bubbling over the falls by my elbow,*
> *cool and still at the far end.*
> *Birds alighting in the basin above the falls,*
> *splashing and drinking gratefully;*
> *the splendor of it all.*
>
> *I sit on my prayer rock and I hear.....*
> *the soft tinkle of the wind chimes*
> *with the occasional gentle breeze;*
> *the birds squawking stridently at each other.*

They are saying "Mine! Mine!"
The soft burbling of the falls as the water
cascades over the rocks;
that pure, underlying silence that remains
before the world is fully awake.
And I imagine that I can hear
the beating of my heart.

I sit on my prayer rock and I smell....
the crisp morning air;
the soft, moist earth
after the evening's rain;
and sometimes, the fragrant wisteria
drooping on the arbor.
But, most of all, the newly minted
freshness of the unbreathed air.
For, on this one morning,
I am the first.

I sit on the prayer rock and now I understand the old saying, "Contentment is not the fulfillment of what you want, but the realization of how much you already have."

So, filled with gratitude for all that I have, I give thanks: for the beauty and spirituality of this garden and with it, the presence of the divine.

You might even call it prayer.

Edna St. Vincent Millay already knew this and in just one sentence captured the essence of my experience.

God, I can push the grass
apart
and lay my finger on Thy
heart.

And that, for me, is mindfulness.

five

Be There Now

Do not be daunted by the world's grief.
Do justly now. Love, mercy now,
Walk humbly now.
You are not obligated to complete the work,
but neither are you free to abandon it."
—from the Talmud

Be There Now

In Christianity, as in Judaism, the fruits of any experience of spiritual awareness are not just internalized but are evidenced in the behavior and acts that follow.

Unless you plan to make a career out of being a navel watcher, you cannot stay on the mountaintop, or in the garden, forever. This has been so succinctly expressed in one of the most frequently quoted passages in Zen:

> *Before enlightenment.......*
> *Chop wood, carry water.*
> *After enlightenment........*
> *Chop wood, carry water.*

Or, in more contemporary terms, as Jack Kornfield, clinical psychologist and Buddhist monk, reminds us with the title of his book, *After the Ecstasy, the Laundry.*

Life goes on. But one's perspectives may shift. For me, that has meant that, in the spirit of mindfulness, I need to truly experience what I encounter in life. Not just the beauty of the earth, but also to experience, with compassion, the beauty and sometimes the suffering. of the earth's inhabitants.

Compassion is part of the credo of my church. At Saint Mark Presbyterian: "We care for all God's children, responding to those in pain and nurturing one another in love."

This is who I strive to be. But, all too often, I realize that I can also be quite adept at walking on the other side of the road. Like most suburbanites, I have been well trained to avoid the hungry and the beggars. "After all," say the experts, "If you give them money they won't get food. They will just go out and buy booze."

Perhaps some of them will. But, for many, there are not a lot of options out there. So I continue to offer a little money with the hope that it will be used for food. And in the meantime, for the small price of a meal, those who eat and those who choose to drink, will both be told: "You matter." And that is food for the soul.

"There, but for the grace of God, go I," were the words my grand-mother, Bobbie, taught me. And from her I learned that God's children might not all be put together in the same way. But they are all of equal value in God's eyes and so should they be in mine.

Bobbie was right. However, sometimes God's children can be quite annoying.

It is the little things that get to me. I remember the time when I was sitting in a church pew on a communion Sunday in the midst of flu season. Next to me sat a developmentally delayed young woman, sneezing and snuffling.

That alone would have been okay. But when she wiped her copi-ously running nose with her open hands and then tightly grasped the loaf of communion bread as it was passed down the pew, I completely forgot what communion was supposed to be about. I just wanted to snatch the bread out of her wet and slippery hands.

"Is she going to massage every single part of that loaf?" I grumped to myself.

And then I looked at her face and the reality hit me. Kind and simple, she wanted only to share in this experience.

So who cares if the bread is now a little shinier then when it started? Here too, is a child of God and she is no less valuable than the CPA sit-ting on the other side of her. And I am quite sure that God didn't mind a bit when I rolled my piece of bread into a small ball and slipped it into my pocket.

Don Quixote would have looked at my pew companion and right away he would have seen only her beauty. Don Quixote of La Mancha was the hero of a story written by Cervantes in the 17th century. He spent his life in an endless pilgrimage devoted to conquering all of the evil in the world.

So endearing is his story that it has been perpetuated in a contemporary version as *The Man of La Mancha,* in which the theme song lauds a hero who could *Dream the Impossible Dream.*

Don Quixote was, of course, considered to be the town fool, as dreamers often are. It didn't help that he did a few nutsy things like tilting at windmills, which he perceived to be enemy monsters.

Most likely, the windmills were Cervantes' symbols of evil on earth. This would make the story a great metaphor for "dreaming the impossible dream," even if one is a bit crazy.

What really made Don Quixote a hero to me and also certified him as quite mad, was the chivalrous, caring side to his nature, which enabled him to see the good in things that others discounted.

Don Quixote could look at people and see an inner beauty that was invisible to the rest of the community. This quality shone in his tender nurture of Aldonza, a local peasant girl, who was rumored to have a less than stellar reputation. Don Quixote saw none of that. He looked at Aldonza and saw only his beautiful "Dulcinea," a grand lady in the vocabulary of the time.

I believe, that like Don, we are called to see the Dulcinea in everyone, perfectly packaged, or not. You may not always know for whom this experience just might be the impetus to look at their own life in a different light.

A client of mine once told me that she was profoundly moved by a single sentence during an AA meeting. That night, after berating herself for being a "loser and totally worthless," a fellow member turned to her and said indignantly, "Look here, "God don't make junk." Scripture points out that recognizing this might just mean doing something about it.

When Jesus is asked, "Who is my neighbor?" he tells the story of the Good Samaritan, the man who does *not* walk on the other side of the road when he passes a wounded man. Rather, he goes to him and binds his wounds. The story ends with the message, "Go and do thou likewise."

Pretty clear. We are all called to be that Samaritan and to bind the wounds of the one in pain. I have come to believe that sometimes "binding the wounds" may just mean listening and valuing that person.

Recently, in one of our pastor's sermons he asked each of us to find our "gift." What is it that we were meant to give? If in doubt, he suggested, we should ask others, "What is my gift?"

Well, I figured it out for myself. I wasn't destined for the great, dynamic, earth-moving things. I will never be a Mother Teresa or a Dietrich Bonhoffer or a Martin Luther King. And that is just as well.

The gift that I have been given is the gift of wanting to listen....... most of the time.

Being attuned to listening can be a part of the mindfulness experience. When you are really aware, it isn't necessary that God speak out loud in words. I believe that you can hear His voice through that pull from within. The pull that says: "Be there now."

I have never felt that to be more real than one night some years ago, when I was in the hospital recovering from some minor surgery.

At the time I had been given some sleep medication —quite a lot in fact. This was due, in large part, to the fact that when the nurse checked my room she found the bed empty. Nurses can get very testy when patients disappear. It looks bad on the charts.

Actually, I had only gone to visit the maternity ward. I love watching the new babies. While I was there I met a young man who was sadly eyeing his infant son. He said his name was Sam. Tall and broad-shouldered, with a tightly curled afro, Sam looked like he belonged on a high school football field, not in a maternity ward.

"I just can't afford one more," Sam said softly, shaking his head in frustration. We talked about a life spent working all day for minimum wage and then returning to a cramped apartment, filled with the noise and clutter of several very young children.

Although I did not live in his world, I began to understand it as we talked. And then, together, we admired his beautiful little boy.

When I finally returned to my room there was an irritated nurse waiting for me with some sleeping pills in a little paper cup. I didn't really need any pills but the nurse needed to have me take them.

Medication usually knocks me out cold. This night started out as no exception. All too soon, after I crawled into bed I began drifting off into La-La Land. Everything was now warm and dark and cozy.

Then faint noises began to penetrate my sleep cocoon. I knew that this was the sound of weeping, but it didn't have anything to do with me. I was not about to leave this sleepy, delicious place. Not yet, anyway.

Gradually, I began to realize that the sobs were coming from the room next door. And, at just about the same time, I also realized that I was needed there. So I dragged out of bed and pulled on my robe, still having no idea what I was going to do when I got there.

It turned out to be pretty simple. I just walked down the hall to the next room, opened the door and walked in. A young woman, actually, she was just a girl, lay face down on the bed, heaving with the sobs that she could not control. I went over and laid my hand on her back.

"Would you like me to stay with you?" I asked. In time, she nodded and, still weeping, shifted over so that I could sit on the edge of the bed. We were together the rest of the night.

The young woman, I'll call her Pat, had just terminated an early, unexpected pregnancy. The baby's father had long since disappeared. Pat's parents were angry, ashamed and "very disappointed" in their daughter. Already, they had abandoned her.

So recently a coed and now en route to becoming a single mother, alone and with no support, Pat had felt that she had no options.

"I just wanted to get the whole thing over with," she confided. Now, Pat could only feel the loss of that tiny, potential new life that had just been scraped from her womb. Tears streamed down her freckled cheeks. Pat twisted her fingers through strands of long, sandy hair and sobbed out her regrets.

"They called it a therapeutic abortion," she cried. "But it wasn't very therapeutic for the baby, was it?" I wanted to shout at her parents and the potential father who had all abandoned her to make her painful choice alone.

The rest of the night we spent together, talking and just being there. When morning came Pat was calmer.

"I feel better now," she said. "Thank you."

I felt better, too and I was no longer even tired. In sharing her story and in our time together, Pat had also given to me. I, too, felt a kind of peace. I believe that there is a healing power in the love that humans share in the caring, one for another. Mother Teresa said it best:

Not all of us can do great things,
but we can all do small things
with great love.

To walk together with someone and share a deeply moving experience is both powerful and draining. For me, it is then necessary that I walk alone for awhile.

So it is not surprising that after being intensely involved in life experiences I can usually be found in the garden. There, I am filled.

I could walk all day through the garden's needle strewn paths. For even with only an acre, in a woodland there is always something to see.

Often the path just leads me right to the cedar garden house. Built with great care by Amish workmen, the house provides a cozy home for a potting table and a big, old rocking chair, not to mention, a secluded hideaway for me. There I can sit quietly with a book of poetry by Mary Oliver, inhale the scent of cedar wood and just let the peace seep in.

The wood burned welcoming sign at the garden house door offers a whimsical greeting. A spin-off from the cartoon strip "Peanuts," the sign informs a new visitor, "The Doctor is in. Advice 5 cents, Listening 10 cents."

And rightly so, listening is twice as valuable as advice. Listening is valuing. It can help us to hear ourselves and sometimes to then begin to see ourselves differently.

The oft-told tale of *The Rabbi's Gift*, by an unknown author, speaks to this very experience of seeing ourselves differently after hearing the words of another.

The Rabbi's Gift

This is a story set in a once great 16th century monastery, located in a beautiful European forest. By the 19th century, decimated by centuries of anti-religious movements and a rise in secularism, the dying monastery was now reduced to one decaying abbey.

All that remained in the Abbey was one old Abbot and four aging monks, who became increasingly discouraged as they prayed together over their declining ministry and about the lack of any interested visitors.

Also in the same forest was an old hut where the Rabbi from a neighboring town would occasionally sequester himself for spiritual renewal.

One day, desperate to save the Abbey, the old Abbot decided to visit the Rabbi and seek his wisdom. He was greeted with warmth and compassion. Together, the men read chapters of the Torah and commiserated over the current lack of spirituality in their communities.

"I have the same problem," said the old Rabbi, "almost nobody goes to Temple anymore."

When it came time to leave, the men hugged each other. The Abbot sighed, "I have failed in my goal. My purpose in coming here was to receive advice from you that would help me to save my dying ministry."

"I am sorry," said the Rabbi. "I wish I had some advice for you. All I can say is that the Messiah is one of you in the Abbey."

When the Abbot returned the monks eagerly crowded around him.

"What did he say?" they chorused.

"He cannot help us," replied the Abbot. We read the Torah together and we prayed. But he had no answers. All he said was that one of you is the Messiah.

In the many months that followed, the monks continued to ask themselves, "What did the Rabbi mean, that one of us is the Messiah? Could that be true? Could it really be one of us? Which one would it be?

Then he must have meant the Abbott," they decided. "He has been our leader for years. But it could have been Brother Thomas. Everyone knows that Thomas is a holy man.

Or would it have been Brother Eldred?" they ponder. "He does get cranky a lot of the time and he sometimes hurts people's feelings. But then, his words can be quite truthful. Maybe it is him.

But surely, the Rabbi did not mean Brother Phillip. He is such a quiet nobody. Yet, he is always there for anyone who needs help. What if he is the Messiah?

Certainly the Rabbi did not mean me. Of course not, I'm just an ordinary person. But what if he did mean me? I couldn't possibly be the Messiah. Could I mean that much to You?"

As the monks reflected on the Rabbi's words, they began to look at each other with a new respect. How could they not value each person who might be the Messiah? Soon a new caring atmosphere began to emerge. The monks began to really listen to each other and to respond thoughtfully.

Now as visitors came to walk through the beautiful forest, they stopped to meditate in the old Abbey. Such was the aura of warmth and respect, that the visitors began to return to pray and talk with the monks. Soon the visitors were bringing their friends to share this special place. Then those friends brought their friends.

When the younger men came to visit this holy place, they stayed to talk with the old monks. As time passed, one after another, many of the young men asked to join the order.

Gradually, the Abbey began to grow and flourish. And so, from the Rabbi's simple words, emerged a new and vibrant spiritual center.

It is just that simple. When you begin to connect with the divine in your life, you are more able to *be here now* in the fullness of life. Then, when the need arises, you will find yourself more able to *be there now.*

six

Square Brown Rooms

*I know that God will not give me
anything I can't handle.
I just wish He didn't trust me
so much.*
—Mother Teresa

Square Brown Rooms

Whether it is people at war with each other, or just within themselves, the healing quality of caring and a listening ear may be the first small step toward peace.

Before I got around to entering graduate school, I found my calling as the Director of The Listening Post, a call-in, walk-in hotline. After running a coffee house and working with youth in crisis, I had a dream of providing a place where kids could just hang out with each other and where those in crisis could always find support.

As I already had a connection working with teens at the local YMCA, that seemed like a logical place to start. So I approached the YMCA Board of Directors with the proposal that we could provide the community with a hotline for teens where anyone who was lonely, hurt or in need could pick up the phone and speak anonymously with another person who would offer supportive caring and, if necessary, a referral to other sources of support.

But, I added, for people who are lonely and need connection in their lives, there is no substitute for a personal encounter. You have only to witness the strength of the AA program to see this in action. The logical answer to youth needs, I suggested, would be to provide a call-in *and* walk-in hotline.

After distributing a copy of the Listening Post proposal to each board member, I launched into an impassioned plea for the YMCA to take this leap into, what was then, uncharted territory and provide a new way to reach kids.

"From my previous youth work," I began, "I already have many community resources: mental health providers, educators, caregivers, juvenile court judges, probation officers, police and potential volunteer staff." These are the kind of details that perk up board members.

"So I know that we can do this," I said, just as if I actually knew what I was talking about. But actually, I did...sort of. There was a nitty-gritty kind of knowledge that did not come from scientifically conducted research, but came from what I had to offer: a lot of experience and a deep feeing of connection with the kids. And the board members responded to that.

"You know, Alice," said one board member, who was an engineer, "you are non-objective and emotionally involved and you present in a style that is halfway between science and religion, but I like what you are saying." So did the rest of the board.

It wasn't long before I found myself with a $5000 start-up grant and a small cadre of teen and adult volunteers. The fledgling Listening Post leased a one bedroom apartment located in a building complex directly across the street from a large shopping mall.

In the beginning it never occurred to me that, without even an advanced degree in the mental health field, perhaps I wasn't "qualified" to direct a call-in, walk-in service that literally took in people off the street. On the other hand, no one else in the community was doing it.

Ignorance is bliss. Neither I nor the YMCA Board suspected that, in addition to a community of solid kids, we would also serve everyone else, from alienated and desperate youth, who considered suicide as their only option, to "drop-outs" from psychiatric institutions, who had been somehow, magically, pronounced cured on exactly the same day that their insurance ran out.

The clientele also included a nineteen year-old, who had a bad habit of walking naked through the street swinging an axe and muttering curses; and the infamous, "mad-ass bomber," who periodically called the help line with the whispered warning, "I'm gonna fuck you in da ass."

Fortunately, we had some on-the-job training to provide support when things got sticky. The Listening Post was blessed with a handful of professionals who volunteered countless hours to our shoestring operation. A psychiatrist, two psychologists, a doctor and two ministers were there for us when we needed them.

They were all excited to be a part of the adventure. And I was excited to learn from them. Soon I found myself with a new dream—to become one of those people to whom I now made referrals. Graduate school was on the agenda.

The teen staff members were getting their own advanced training, learning about listening skills and referral sources. But the most heated discussions were around the topics of public relations and promotions.

A flyer was designed and distributed to area high schools. The really big issue was around stickers. Everyone concurred that we *must* have stickers. After much debate, a Band-Aid size sticker was designed with the simple message: "The Listening Post – We care. Can we help?" In the amount of time the staff spent discussing the selection of those eight words I could have read an entire novel.

Everyone was pleased with the results and soon all the local high schools were sprouting stickers everywhere. Unfortunately, some of the stickers were placed in less appropriate public places, which may account for some of the bizarre calls we received.

The youth staff soon became a welcoming community. Almost immediately the "Post" provided a friendly fellowship where teenagers could drop by because they were lonely or would just like someplace where they would be welcomed.

People also came because they were happy and would like to share that feeling with a friend. The oft-repeated message of this caring community was: "When you come to the Listening Post you enter as a friend. Pass it on to the next person."

Sadly, we discovered that sometimes in life, all the caring in the world is not enough. Never was that more evident then when Olsen, shy, intelligent and highly sensitive, but most of all, our friend, took his own life in the beginning of his college freshman year.

Only in retrospect, did the kids realize that they had never really known Olsen. He had remained a silent presence with a shy smile. But Olsen had lived in a shadow of pain and anger that his family and the friends who cared for him could not share. Nor could his doctors reach him.

When Olsen finally did reach out it was in a phone call that I will never forget.

"I-uh, have-uh problem," said a weak, little voice on the other end of the line. "I just took a whole bottle of aspirin....I can feel it coming over me now…"

"Where are you, Olsen?" I asked, recognizing his voice. Thank God I had come home early that Tuesday night.

"It doesn't really matter," answered the flat voice. "It doesn't really make any difference at all…. No one cares anyway…. I just didn't want to die all alone and have no one know about it……I wanted to tell you about it."

"I'm so glad you did, Olsen. I'll be right with you. Where are you?"

"Well-l… I'm, uh, at the mall shopping center at the drug store."

After racing to the drug store, I spotted Olsen right away. He was a dejected, raggedy bundle slouched against the drug counter as the shoppers passed by, seemingly unaware of the tragedy unfolding in front of them.

"Hey," I slid in next to him. "I'm glad you waited." Olsen just looked at me with dull eyes that looked too old and too weary. No tears left.

"Tell me about it."

"Everybody is better off without me," he mumbled, looking at the counter.

"Even if that were true, Olsen and I can't buy it. *You* certainly wouldn't be better off, huh?

"Who cares?"

"I do, for one and even more important, so should you." Olsen just shrugged.

"Let's talk about it in the car," I suggested, "so I can get you to a doctor and make sure that you're safe first."

"No."

"Look, if you decide that you want to die, Olsen, I can't stop you. Nobody can. But, suppose you decide that you want to live? Then it's too late. You can always get dead later. But you can't ever get un-dead. And I think that you're too precious to lose."

He wavered. I took him firmly by the arm. (You can't always be non-directive.) And we went to the hospital.

At the hospital an efficient nurse whisked Olsen off for the routine ministrations and returned to interrogate me for the usual paperwork.

Olsen's parents were out of town and were called for permission to take any necessary procedures to rid his system of the toxic drugs.

While his parents raced back to town, I remained at the hospital feeling overwhelmed and inadequate. Desperately, I wished that I had the intensive training and wisdom to handle this crisis.

The nurse, who was probably younger than I, but who looked as if she had seen everything twice already, asked disinterestedly how many aspirin I thought Olsen had *really* taken.

"You know," she confided, "how adolescents *are.*" I wanted to tell her that I probably knew more than she did about how adolescents *are.*

Instead, I sat down with an elderly copy of *Life* magazine and thought how great it would be if hospital emergency rooms could have some kind of compassionate and well-trained, or even just compassionate, volunteers who would be available to help in times of need like this.

It would be nice, too, I thought, if there were someone around for me. In situations like this I often felt this great sense of inadequacy and a real need for someone with whom to share the worry and the responsibility. Someone, I wished, who would have all kinds of strength, understanding and wisdom..

"You can go in and see Olsen now," said a white-coated doctor who rushed by on his way to another crisis. He steered me to one of the small treatment rooms and en route, provided a rapid status report.

"Owen's stomach has been emptied but he still has a toxic blood level," said the doctor. " We are going to admit him overnight as soon as his parents arrive to sign the papers."

Olsen lay on one of the examination tables, looking tired and old. Only the smooth face gave away his age.

"They don't really pump your stomach," he volunteered weakly. "They just make you puke until it's empty. He smiled just a little around the edges. I felt saggy with relief, just knowing that he was safe again.

But, Olsen was *not* safe again. Nor would he ever be. He was unable to rise above a depression that said there was nothing ahead that was going to make life any better.

"My parents kept asking 'What happened?' Olsen later recounted. *Nothing* happened that day that was different than any other day. Nothing. That was it, nothing. It *was* like every other day and I just couldn't stand it, knowing that it was always going to be like that."

In the weeks that followed, Olsen continued to deteriorate. The signs were all there. Beneath that innocent, boyish face that had once smiled shyly under an unruly sheath of light brown hair, another Olsen began to emerge as an angry, distant and withdrawn boy.

I knew that Olsen needed more than I, or the Listening Post could give him. It was time to reconnect with his parents. Once again notified, Olsen's parents arranged for, what they assumed to be, the best psychiatric care available. The trouble was, these "experts" were not giving Owen what he needed either.

From the start of psychotherapy, Olsen was unhappy with his doctor, who he experienced as distant and condescending. At first, Olsen would return to the Listening Post following a therapy session and jokingly recount the interactions of that hour. Once, Olsen bragged, he had successfully angered the psychiatrist by questioning his credentials and competence.

"You're just a spoiled brat," responded the doctor. "If you were my kid I'd beat you right now." And that pretty much defined their therapeutic alliance.

As the weeks passed, Olsen's joking ceased and he began to withdraw more frequently. Soon, he rarely spoke at the Listening Post. Instead, he began to call me at home. Increasingly, Olsen aired grievances toward his family and friends, who he now felt were slighting him and talking behind his back. But that didn't bother him anymore, he insisted, for he was now becoming more like a computer.

"You are the only one I trust," Olsen confided. "Sometimes I wonder what it would have been like to have a mother like you. I think I would have broken her." Increasingly, his comments focused on the meaninglessness of life and the belief that a lot of people, including himself, "would be better off dead."

My own anxiety level was mounting. I knew that Olsen was decompensating and paranoid. To me it seemed that he was becoming a threat to himself and others. But I was unable to convince anyone else that this was becoming a dangerous situation.

The mental health professionals had been notified that Olsen's mental state was rapidly deteriorating. His parents had also been informed. The police were not yet an option because no direct threats had been validated.

Knowing that I could no longer handle this situation by myself, I turned, in desperation, to Ruth, who was my Listening Post. Ruth was a retired psychologist and the leading force in a citizen's watchdog group that monitored the activities in the county's juvenile court system. In that capacity, she had taken a great interest in my work with the youth of the Listening Post.

As our friendship developed, Ruth had become more than just a mentor, who provided insight and support. Somewhere along the way she had become a guardian angel who guided me through all the tight spots.

With a youthful naivete, I never feared for myself. Love, I believed, conquered everything. Ruth did not share this belief. Consequently, she spent considerable energy protecting me from myself.

It was Ruth who had first recognized Olsen's potential danger to others as well as to himself. Several times she warned me that his feelings for me were not healthy and to avoid ever being alone with him.

Because the tragedy at Columbine had yet to happen, no one at the Listening Post ever took Olsen's joking references to his supposed hobby of bomb building to be a serious concern. Ruth did and she was later to remind us of this. But, one afternoon at the Listening Post, when Olsen announced that he now had a gun and was going to kill his parents, there were no longer any options left.

The police and Olsen's parents were notified. When he arrived home that afternoon, Olsen was met by two police officers, who, upon finding a knife in his jacket pocket, handcuffed and delivered him to a youth detention facility to await a juvenile court appearance, which would then have placed him in a psychiatric hospital.

This was to have been a successful step toward recovery. Instead, it was only the prelude to the unfolding tragedy. Unfortunately, a young, idealistic, but ignorant, probation officer was assigned Olsen's case before the court hearing. The officer decided to spare this "nice, young boy" from the trauma of court and hospitalization. Instead of a court hearing, Olsen was returned to a foster placement and outpatient counseling.

All too soon, Olsen was back at the Listening Post, now feeling betrayed and spewing angry messages. He presented me with a "hate book," in which he laid out his rage at both the staff and me. I read the words, which would later haunt me: "People are mutilated by you. You are all phonies. Are you satisfied now? You've destroyed my life." The book was followed up with a call to notify me that I would be better off dead.

Now there was no longer a choice. The risk was too great. The court and the mental health professionals had failed both Olsen and us.

Sadly, I contacted Olsen to explain that although we still cared deeply about him, he would no longer be allowed to return to the Listening Post. Devastated, Olsen howled out his grief and shouted out curses that I would be better off dead.

The next night Olsen called one of the youth staff at home and said that now the Listening Post would have to close "and the only way for that to happen would be to kill Alice."

The following afternoon an adult staff member answered a call on the Listening Post phone. Puzzled by the silence on the line, he was about to hang up when he heard the slow, steady sound like a clock in the background: "Tick...Tick...Tick."

By now my concern had jumped from anxiety to panic. Knowing that the police and the courts no longer considered Olsen to be a legitimate threat, I realized that they were no longer an option for support. So, once again, I turned to *my* listening post, Ruth.

At first, Ruth just listened as I poured out my fears for what might happen next and my sadness for Olsen, who was so broken. Not once did Ruth point out how I might have handled things differently. Then, together, we decided that it was time to take action. And already I felt safer and stronger.

In retrospect, I believe that Henri Nouwen, the Catholic priest and theologian, might have been describing what I experienced with Ruth, when he defined a supporting friendship:

> *When we honestly ask ourselves which person in our lives means the most to us we often find that it is those who, instead of giving advice, solutions or cures, have chosen rather to share our pain and touch our wounds with a warm and tender hand. The friend who can be silent with us in a moment of despair or confusion, who can stay with us in an hour of grief or bereavement, who can tolerate not*

knowing, not curing, not healing and face with us the reality of our powerlessness, that is a friend who cares.

Much later, after the tragedy was over, a staff member commented, "Alice, you came so close to being killed. You must have had a guardian angel watching over you." I did. Her name was Ruth.

And so, as Ruth and I had decided, I called Olsen's psychiatrist. After identifying myself, I explained that Olsen was a crisis waiting to happen.

"I can't discuss Olsen with you," snapped the doctor.

" I understand confidentiality," I answered. "You don't have to share any information with me and you can tell Olsen everything I say. But you need to know that Olsen is a serious threat to himself and others. He is on the brink. Please listen......"

Click. The slam of the doctor's phone was my answer.

Two weeks later, Olsen was found, alone in his dorm room, a worn brown leather belt wrapped tightly around his neck as he hung limply from a pipe in the ceiling.

The police reported that apparently Olsen had been very determined to die, for it appeared that he had made two previous unsuccessful attempts to hang himself. It was the third and final try that had broken his neck. So great was his desperation that this time he had chosen to die alone.

"It's not your fault. It's not your fault," Ruth kept reminding me as I sobbed over the phone when the news of Owen's death reached me at the Listening Post. "He was just too damaged and his pain was too great. You did everything you could.".

"But it wasn't enough," I cried, stumbling over my "if onlys."

"No," said Ruth, "it wasn't, because the system broke down and Owen didn't want to live anymore." She stayed with me until I could shoulder my own grief and be there for the youth staff and friends as the word spread and they came stumbling in to share the horror and the pain.

Later that evening, Bob, an Episcopal priest, joined our group as we all sat on the floor in a grief circle. We held hands and shared our sorrow, until finally we could also talk about the earlier days and the good times we had had with Olsen.

We cried and talked about how angry we were that he had done this to himself – and to us. And we talked about learning to forgive Olsen because we loved him. Bob reminded us, once again, that although we had given love, Olsen was just unable to let it in.

So, we cried together, as the group that couldn't reach Olsen in life, supported each other instead. I will always remember Bob's words in his closing prayer: "Olsen who was so broken, now is whole.."

In the weeks that followed, the Listening Post youth continued to grieve for the loss of their friend. Many hours were spent discussing life and death and loss. There were a few kids who saw Olsen's death as a courageous stand against the cruelty of life.

It was after several continued discussions that the kids were able to conclude that having the courage to walk through pain and build a better life is the greater choice. And so, The Listening Post poetry book was born.

Everyone agreed that what they wanted most to remember about Olsen was not just the pain but his other side, the gentle, tender personality, which he had once shared with us.

In honor of Olsen's memory, his grieving parents requested that, in lieu of flowers, contributions be made to The Listening Post community, which had always been dear to his heart. The youth chose to use those contributions to create and publish their own poetry book, in which they were able to talk about their feelings, instead of acting on them.

One youth staff member eloquently expressed her experience with Olsen's death in words that spoke to all of us:

To Olsen

Two worlds went by – spinning
Yours and mine –
And suddenly, for a short time –
they slowed down, touched and
We became friends.

46 | Alice G. Miller, PhD

But is was a long time that i
Sat and wondered if you would
let me in – let me care about you.
And for a long time there – i think you did.
Now I sit in disbelief
remembering your shy eyes
and gentle way –
I don't know how I feel – or
if i will ever understand –
maybe someday when i stop
hurting.

My world is now spinning to
new times
i can only wonder where your
world is taking you –
and hope that whatever you
searched for – is now found.

–Alana

Two other Listening Post teens contributed the poem, *Square Brown Rooms*, whose author was unknown. "Because," one of the contributors said, "that boy speaks for me."

Square Brown Rooms

He always wanted to explain things,
But no one cared.
So he drew.
Sometimes he would draw and it wasn't anything.
He wanted to carve it in stone or write it in the sky.
He would lie out in the grass and look up at the sky
And it would be only the sky and him and the things inside him
that needed saying.
And it was after that he drew the picture.
It was a beautiful picture.
He kept it under his pillow and would let no one see it.

And he would look at it every night and think about it.
And when it was dark, and his eyes were closed, he could still see it.
And it was all of him
And he loved it.
When he started school he brought it with him.
Not to show anyone, but to have it with him like a friend.
It was funny about school.
He sat in a square, brown desk
Like all the other square brown desks
And he thought it should be red
And his room was a square brown room,
Like all the other square brown rooms
And it was tight and close.
And stiff.
He hated to hold the pencil and chalk
With his arm stiff and his feet flat on the floor.
Stiff.
With the teacher watching and watching.
The teacher came and spoke to him.
She told him to wear a tie like all the other boys.
He said he didn't like them.
And she said it didn't matter.
After that they drew.
And he drew all yellow and it was how he felt about Morning.
And it was beautiful.
The teacher came and smiled at him.
"What's this," she said, "why don't you do something like Ken's
Isn't that beautiful?"
After that his mother bought him a tie.
And he always drew airplanes and rocketships like everyone else..
And he threw the old picture away.
And when he lay alone looking at the sky
It was big and blue and all of everything,
But he wasn't anymore.
He was square inside
And brown
And his hands were stiff

And he was like everyone else.
And the things inside him that needed saying, didn't need it anymore.
It had stopped pushing
It was crushed
Stiff.
Like everything else.

This anonymous poem was originally submitted to a 12th grade English teacher two weeks before the student committed suicide. Unlike the young author of this poem, The Listening Post teenager who submitted this poem was able to share his feelings and then get the help that he needed.

And, as for me, now I too, knew what I needed. It was time to return to graduate school and become the social worker that my heart had already led me to be.

Sometimes, as our youth discovered, it takes more courage to live than to die. That is why The Listening Post poetry book was titled, *I Believe in Me.* And that is why the book was dedicated, not just to the memory of a death – but to the spirit of life.

seven

Finding Peace for the Spider Woman

The first duty of love is to listen.

—Paul Tillich

Finding Peace for the Spider Woman

It was that same spirit of life that prompted the call from the "Spider Woman."

"I don't know the reason for calling you," said a tiny voice on the other end of the line. Although it has been a long time since I received that call, I have never forgotten it, or the little girl who ultimately made such an impact on my life.

At the Listening Post we got a lot of calls like that. But they were never the same. And you never got used to it. This time it was the "Spider Woman."

I recognized her voice as soon as she spoke. Which personality, I wondered, would she use today: "Susan " or "Honey" or "Jan." It didn't matter. They were all the same lonely, frightened, hurting, little 13-year old girl who, when things got too tough, picked up the phone and called a hotline number.

"I keep hurting myself," she whispered. "I want to get rid of myself."

We talked about that for a long time. You do not just make immediate referrals with people like the "Spider Woman." Because, all too often, they experience the referral as a rejection. Instead, you listen to them, walk with them and care about them until they are ready to take another step.

"It doesn't matter, no one cares anyway," she kept repeating.

"I care what happens to you," I let her know during the conversation.

"Don't say that!" she drew in her breath sharply. "My friend, Karen said that once, but she didn't mean it. She rejected me, too.

"How do I know you mean it?"

"Well, I can see how you'd feel that way if you've been hurt before," I agreed, thinking out loud. "But look, I give you my time. And that's like little pieces of my life. I couldn't do that if I didn't care about you." She bought that. I thought about it some more.

"But maybe you need to hear me tell you," I added. "Hey, I'll let you know, too." And that made us both feel good.

Soon, the "Spider Woman," asked to be called "Honey," and began to talk about her life. In the months that followed, several of us at the Listening Post continued to talk with Honey and fell in love with this tough, scared, impish, belligerent and yet, somehow, tender little girl. At times here was so much anger boiling up in Honey that she would strike out in wild verbal assaults and threats.

"I'm going to beat the shit out of you!" she promised me regularly. Other times, Honey would just wander off in a world of fantasy. It was easier to deal with the anger.

"I'm coming over there and I'm going to beat the hell out of you!" Honey warned me one afternoon. I wondered, idly, how big she was.

"That would be difficult," I reminded her, "because I don't fight."

"I'll smash you hard and make you fight me back," she threatened, loudly.

"I suppose that would probably knock me over," I admitted. "But then what are you going to do? I won't hit you back. Now how are you going to win a fight with someone who isn't fighting? I followed with some of my thoughts about non-violence.

"You make me sick!" screamed Honey.

"Why?"

"Because you are loveable. I want to be just like you and I can't, so you make me sick!"

"Hey, you're just like *you*," I reminded her, "and that's nice, too.

Maybe when you like yourself better, then I won't make you sick."

As we spent more hours talking, a deep mutual trust built up between Honey and me. But it was a trust based on two people caring a great deal about each other, but not on many facts. I was still never exactly sure where truth left off and fantasy began with Honey. And sometimes, I was beginning to realize, neither was she.

Honey's world, as she shared it with me, was full of wild people, drugs, violence and pain. But woven through all the fantasy there seemed to be a bittersweet underlay of truth.

By this time, I knew that Honey had grown up in the inner city as the unplanned and unwelcomed baby of a 13-year old mother. Her earliest memories were of being shuttled around and dumped by a child mother, who saw her baby as a doll to be picked up and discarded on a whim.

Much later, these truths were verified by Honey's harried, young grandmother, who contacted me, only after much prompting from Honey. Her own daughter, confided the grandmother, had given birth to Honey at age 13 and had never been a very "reliable" mother.

Now, as a grandmother, she expressed deep regret that she, herself, also had been a very young mother who had always had to work for long hours. Consequently, her own daughter, and now her young granddaughter had often been left alone to fend for themselves. Although remorseful, the grandmother was unwilling to get involved or to share any more information, other than to add that Honey was now pretty much on her own. Overworked and swamped, as the city's social services workers were, it did not seem that they were about to be able locate any better placement for Honey, when she still had a mother and grandmother who, in their own way, cared about her.

Honey's life was one long series of destructive experiences. For now, the anguish was more than she could endure. But, I did not know that then. I only knew that she was retreating more and more into a world of fantasy. My friend, Honey, was replaced by "Jan."

Jan wanted to play games and she talked a lot about sadism and brutality. Sometimes, she talked about her baby. Jan's baby was a beautiful, little boy who lived with his kindly grandmother. Every weekend, said Jan, she visited his grandmother and played with her little baby. On bad days, Jan would tell me that she wished her baby was dead.

Then one day Jan told me that she knew Susan, too. Susan had been a good friend of hers. Now it seemed that Susan was dying.

"She doesn't want to do anything but lie there and suffer," said Jan. "Susan thinks that she has done something wrong and has to be punished."

I suggested that it seemed to me that Susan needed to be loved.

"Yes," agreed Jan solemnly, but it was too late for that now. Susan was not willing to try anymore. "And," she added, "Susan wouldn't let me to come to visit her."

The next daily call I received was from a very distraught Jan, informing me that Susan was dead and had disappeared. When she spoke of this it was with very real terror. Then the terror changed to anger, focused on me.

"Alice, thanks to you, Susan is dead," she told me in a tone of bitter accusation. "And it's not my fault at all. It's all your fault." And I hurt for the pain in her voice.

"Hey," I said gently, "It doesn't have to be my fault in order for it not to be your fault. We stayed there, silently on the phone together, until she began to cry softly.

"No, it's my fault," she sobbed. I went away and left her all alone... ...I don't understand anything anymore....I have a feeling that I'm going to be next.......it's so terrible....

I left her knowing that I was going to be sticking with her, which didn't seem like a heck of a lot at the time. But it was all I had to offer. In retrospect, with many more years of experience and considerably more training, I realize that it was, indeed, a lot. However, then I just felt humbled by the enormity of her need and my own sense of inadequacy.

It was then that I made the decision to return for additional training and to become one of "those" people to whom we were always trying to make referrals. But, my immediate problem was to find one of "those" referrals now.

Then I remembered that Honey had once mentioned having a few visits with a psychologist in a government clinic. He had made quite an impression on her.

"My doctor taught me to be honest with myself and with other people," Honey had recalled proudly, "I try not to lie anymore."

Right then I had put that doctor's name down as someone worth knowing. Suddenly, this seemed like a very good time to call him. Using a telephone book, with Honey's phonetic spelling of his last name, it took me a couple pages of psychologists to locate Dr. T.

"I need to gain some understanding," I told Dr. T, who had since gone into private practice and was not taking new referrals. Right away, he remembered Honey.

"This little girl really concerns me," I told him. I already knew that she was disassociating, but was she also schizophrenic or a fantastic liar?

"Possibly all three," suggested Dr. T. He concurred with my gut feeling that I should risk and confront Honey in a gentle way, with her presentation of a multiple identity. Somehow, he helped me to feel supported, sensitive and wise enough to do it in a way that Honey could handle.

The next time Honey called I just did it, with as much simplicity and honesty as I could. There was a long silence, which I just quietly shared with Honey.

"Is there something wrong with me?," she finally whispered.

"I think that you need some help to deal with the things that cause you pain," I told her. And then we talked about some of the things that were right with her.

Suddenly, she was babbling……"important to me…..pieces of my life….." she rambled incoherently, "What can I do…..what do you want…." she lapsed into fragments of past memories.

"Don't worry about that now," I said very slowly. Let's just start with right now. What is your real name?"

Catching her breath and hesitating, almost as if to release that name would be to risk losing all the defenses that she had built up, Honey swallowed and blurted very clearly, "Susan Mary —"

"Thank you, Susan," I whispered, tears coming to my eyes. "Oh, thank you for trusting me."

Because Susan had asked me what I wanted from her and had given at great risk I asked her the same question.

"What would you like from me, Susan?"

"Caring," she whispered after a pause. "And help, I think. What kind I don't know."

"The caring you already have," I told her. "And we'll start looking for the help together." And, for several months, that is what we did, while we waited for Susan to be willing to take the next step for a referral. As "Honey" and "Jan" diminished, Susan and I talked daily and built a new relationship based on honesty.

"You can tell me anything you want and I'll listen," I promised. "You don't have to dress it up or change it around. If it's important to you I will want to hear it." We talked about psychiatric help, but Susan was still wary.

"Sometime when you are ready to think about it again," I suggested, "you can let me know."

As the weeks went on, Susan shared that no one had ever listened to her before. Now, in our daily calls, she was beginning to understand that the traumas that she had experienced were just that – traumas. She was not to blame for things that had happened to her, nor did they define her. Instead, we looked at the incredible strength that she had already demonstrated and how that strength was a piece of what already defined her.

To throw a diagnosis of a serious mental disorder aside for a moment, I would speculate that within Susan there still remained a strong core self that could ultimately integrate her own sense of identity and avoid the need to split off what had been too painful to bear.

As we talked, I learned how painful her earlier life had been for Susan. An unhappy, disturbed and abandoned child to begin with, she had been further unsettled by her young mother's marriage to a new husband and the subsequent birth of a baby sister who, Susan felt, usurped any place she might have had in the family.

Then came the trauma of being raped by a 28-year old uncle. To compound the tragedy, no one in the family believed Susan's story and treated it as a sign of mental illness. Only when her ensuing pregnancy became quite obvious did the family voice any concern over her condition.

During her eighth month of pregnancy Susan was once again raped by her uncle. This time the water broke and she was raced to the hospital where she delivered a baby boy by Cesarean section. The uncle by now had disappeared, but the family continued to maintain his innocence.

The hospital staff, who should have known better, ignored Susan's decision to place the baby for adoption. Instead, they" proceeded to fuss over the infant, insisting that Susan should hold her "dear little baby." She received no support in placing the baby for adoption and walked out of the hospital with a burden of guilt that no 13-year old victim should ever have to endure. These were the tortured weeks when Susan had first resorted to a world of fantasy.

For Susan, the trauma only increased. When she returned to school, the kids bullied and teased her about her past pregnancy and the baby she "gave away." One day, when she could take no more,

Susan left her school and called the Listening Post. Through tears, she begged me to come and get her.

When I met her at a dingy pancake house, all Susan could talk about was running away forever. At that point she began suggesting that death would be such an easy way out.

"Susan, if the pain is so bad then, instead of running away, why not run to something?" I offered. And that was the beginning of our search for a mental health placement.

After a lengthy phone conversation, Susan's young mother and her new husband reluctantly agreed to meet us at a Prince Georges County hospital to arrange for a psychiatric evaluation and placement. We arrived at the hospital with Susan's family in tow and full of bright hopes that this would be the beginning of supportive therapy for Susan.

Four-and-a-half hours later that hope was somewhat tarnished, as we sat, still waiting, in the emergency room. The doctor, a young psychiatry resident (I would have flunked him, myself) said that Susan was most definitely suicidal.

The doctor spent almost his entire time with Susan avidly discussing the relative merits of different methods of suicide. I'm sure that he probably provided her with some methods that she had not yet considered. It began to appear that this discussion was meeting some morbid interest of his own.

Concluding the examination, the doctor then remembered that, in spite of the fact that Susan was at great risk, she was, after all, only 13 years old. Sorry, he added, but this hospital did not admit mental patients who were less than 15 years old. He had absolutely no idea of any other possible placements. So good-bye.

It was now past midnight and just when I thought it couldn't get any worse, Susan's mother and her husband announced that they were really sorry but they had better leave as he had to get up early for work. But, they agreed that if I thought that she should be in a hospital, that would be okay with them.

This was not the time to give these two the answer they deserved. Susan was just sitting hunched over on the bench and quietly falling apart. I held her hand and reassured her that I would stick with her and we would find another place. Inside, I was not feeling quite so confident. What does one do in the middle of the night alone with a suicidal child, no parents and no money?

Finally, after a few emergency phone calls, I was able to get a staff psychiatrist from a Montgomery County hospital out of bed. Sympathetic to our plight, he agreed to meet us first thing in the morning to arrange for an emergency admittance to the hospital's psychiatric unit.

Susan spent the remaining few hours of the night with a kind family from our church. They would never consider it a big deal to be awakened in the early morning hours to provide comfort and a bed to a scared, little girl.

Bright and early the next morning, I drove Susan to be admitted to the hospital. Because the kind doctor arranged all the paperwork, we somehow got her admitted without any parental presence or discussion of payment. (There was to be hell to pay for this later.) But, for now, I breathed a great sigh of relief. Susan was safe and that, I thought, was that.

Far from it. From the time Susan arrived on the ward I began to get calls from that unit's psychiatrist, inquiring as to when she would be leaving. It seemed that Susan was hearing voices telling her to jump out the window. She was also "acting out." Sometimes, they reported, she was aggressive and loud. Other times she was withdrawn and refused to talk with the psychiatrist.

I tried pointing out that these behaviors were to be expected on a psych unit. But my suggestions were not well received. However, they were more than happy to hear that I would be coming in to see Susan.

When I arrived at the hospital it was a very subdued Susan who greeted me. Clearly, she was heavily medicated. The remainder of the time she was confined to the unit's front room because she had cut her leg and wrist in a suicide attempt. And this was the girl they wanted to release?

"I guess you wondered why you even bothered to put me here?" mumbled Susan, as I sat beside her on the lounge couch.

"No, I know why I put you here. I care about you and I want you to have the help you need." Susan was silent for a moment.

"I know," she answered finally. "I told them I was going to run away. But I won't do it, for your sake."

58 | Alice G. Miller, PhD

"I'm glad." There's a mental health type answer that goes, "No, you need to do this for your *own* sake." But Susan's ego was pretty fragile at this point. Wanting to do something for me was a positive sign of reaching out and I *was* glad.

As I sat on the couch, deep in thought, Susan stood behind me with her comb and silently braided my long hair in a gesture of touching and affection.

Inside, I just wanted to cry. Would no one take a chance on this sensitive girl who had hurt so much and yet, who had such inner drive and strength? Why couldn't they just support her as she acted out all the pain and anger and help her to deal with it?

However, the hospital administrators were not focused on treatment. They were having some anxiety issues of their own. It did not appear that Susan was going to be a paying patient and her parents clearly were choosing not to be involved. So they, unofficially, appointed me as her guardian.

This was not an honorary position. They wanted her out and they needed someone to pressure. I was equally determined that they were not going to get away with dumping her.

"I'll find a better place for you, Susan," I promised. "Where now?" became the question at the Listening Post. We contacted numerous mental health facilities to find a place that would take a suicidal 13-year old girl. She was too old for Hillcrest and too young for Prince Georges Hospital, too poor for the private facilities.

Unfortunately she was not from an "intact biological family unit for the current NIMH, National Institute of Mental Health Center program. And certainly, she was too valuable to be warehoused at the state hospital. But, the amazing thing is, that when you keep trying, there is always a loophole somewhere.

Our loophole turned up practically in Susan's back yard. The, then Washington, D. C. mental health program, under the sponsorship of NIMH, had developed an adolescent program at St. Elizabeth's Hospital that was free to residents of the District of Columbia.

So, at last, under the sponsorship of NIMH, Susan would be enrolled in a program with individual and group therapy, schooling, three sessions a week with a psychiatrist and psychodrama sessions.

As an added bonus, this, hopefully, was a program with enough clout to get the necessary police involvement to locate and put away her uncle, the man who had so traumatized her life. Wow! This is our tax dollar at work. But, most of all, this was the start of a new beginning for Susan.

Soon afterwards, there was also a new beginning for me. I returned to graduate school and eventually to a Social Work doctorate program. After leaving the Listening Post, I became the director of a residential treatment program and finally on to private practice.

Some of the youth I have seen throughout my practice have been in painful, hurting places, much like Susan was. And now, more than ever, I realize that although skill and training are valuable assets, there is no rehabilitation tool more powerful than human caring.

Recently, a client asked me how I had made the career decision to become a psychotherapist.

"Well," I smiled, remembering a long ago phone call, "it all began with a boy named Olsen....and a call from the Spider Woman."

eight

An Instrument of Peace

*"Human Beings are
God's Language."*
—Menachen Mendel

An Instrument of Peace

Sometimes the sheer ordinariness of a life well lived obscures the beauty of the great gift that one life brought to this world. That is how it was with Linda Miller.

No one outside of Lehigh Valley, Pennsylvania ever heard of Linda, with the exception of me, because I was her sister-in-law. She had worked at a perfectly ordinary job with Pennsylvania Power and Light. She was never on television. She never invented anything and she never ran for public office.

And yet, when Linda died recently and all too soon, the funeral had to be delayed for over an hour, because the line of mourners waiting to greet the family kept streaming through. The church parking lot overflowed and vans were hustled into service to ferry people from the parking lot of a neighboring church.

So why all this fuss over someone who never really did anything extraordinary? Maybe because she really was just an ordinary person, like the rest of us. An ordinary person with a great big heart, who seemed to touch everyone she met. No big deal. She just cared a lot.

Linda was not larger than life, she *was* life. Never was that more apparent than in her death when we, who all took her for granted, suddenly saw the gap left by her passing.

"I do nothing remarkable," Linda once told her pastor, after completing another of the myriad tasks that keep a church's ministry flowing.

"I do what needs to be done. Someone else could have done it, but I did it." No big deal. But it was a big deal. Linda was always there for someone with a need. And that pretty much sums up how Linda viewed her life. No big deal.

She was not super cute or super pretty, unless you count that warm smile. But she was better than super pretty. Linda had grace, that indescribable quality of the spirit of God acting through man.

Pretty doesn't last. Grace does.

When I first met Linda I was a nervous young bride-to-be, hoping to impress my future in-laws. This did not turn out to be a Hallmark moment. But Linda, even then, managed to sweeten the deal.

My first impression of Linda was of a shy, appealing little girl lost in the shuffle of four brothers. To me it seemed like a whole lot of boys and a whole lot of noise.

Little "strubble kopf," her father called her. The Pennsylvania German translation means something like "messy hair" or "tousle head." I *think* it was a term of endearment.

Linda smiled and smiled that day, while her parents gamely tried to hide their disappointment that their future daughter-in-law was neither Pennsylvania German nor much of a cook. To make matters worse she was not even particularly interested in housekeeping —a domestic zero! At this point even two out of three wouldn't have been bad.

It was a difficult time for Stan's parents. They had had such high hopes that their first born – the golden boy – would have fared better in the marriage lottery. Or, at the very least, he could have found a local girl who displayed even a minimal interest in housewifely skills instead of reading or roaming through the woods.

However, for the golden boy it was a case of "the heart wants what the heart wants," as Woody Allen once said, under much less favorable circumstances. So my future in-laws graciously tried to accept that their hope for redemption was turning out to be a lost cause.

"Welcome to the family," Stan's father finally managed. His mother disappeared into the other room. Now I, too, was feeling like a lost cause.

So when little "strubble kopf" opened her arms to me it felt like instant belonging. What a gift! And when I departed from that first scary visit it was Linda who scrunched up to me and whispered:

"Aw-w-w, don't go. I was just getting used to you."

Funny thing, little "strubble kopf" grew up to be a warm, caring woman, who never did consider cooking and cleaning to be much of a priority. I like to think that I helped to corrupt her.

Never would Linda turn down a dinner invitation that would allow her to avoid cooking a meal. And always, there would be spontaneous "runs" to the ice cream store with a van full of nieces and nephews. Never mind the dust balls accumulating on the stairs.

Priorities. I like that in a woman.

One big priority for Linda was celebrating life and making dreams come true, her own and others. Following the Philadelphia Phillies was one of Linda's quirkier priorities. This was *her* team.

Never mind that the Phillies were the only major league team to lose over ten thousand games. Win or lose, Linda rewarded the Phillies with the same fierce loyalty that she held for family and friends.

Twelve years before her death, Linda gave herself the treat of a lifetime and paid to be on the Phillies "Dream Team." That spring, after weeks of rigorous training, Linda traveled to Florida for a week of "Spring Training" with the Phillies coaches and staff. As the only woman, Linda got to socialize with the players and become the catcher for her team.

Sometimes dreams come true just because someone takes the initiative to make them happen. And that was the message that Linda imprinted on her own nieces and nephews.

But, sometimes dreams don't materialize. Or, at least, not the way we planned them. Life doesn't always deal you the hand that you expected or hoped for. Linda was no exception.

The young woman, who wished to have a long marriage and a loving family with several children, had only a brief marriage and no children.

Her husband was a shy, gentle young man, who initially responded to Linda's warm and nurturing spirit. Quite possibly, he was looking for another mother. However, he already had one and she was not about to relinquish the throne.

Although, in his own way, her husband loved Linda, when life presented him with a decision to make, he ultimately decided that he preferred living happily ever after – with mom.

So Linda was never blessed with biological children of her own. But she did end up with children aplenty. First, there were her niece

Finding Peace In Our Thyme | 65

and nephews, who were then followed by their own children. Linda loved them all as if they were her own. And so they were.

The loving embodiment of Mother Teresa's answer to the first step toward world peace: "Go home and love your family," Linda passed on the values of nurture and caring to the next generation. And she did it all with joy and playfulness.

Lindsey, at age seven, mourned the loss of her great aunt and vowed to grow up and be "just like Linda." Now, as a teenager, Lindsey is already the kind of capable, self-assured young woman, who will doubtless leave her own mark on the world. And, in so doing, Lindsey becomes another piece of Linda's legacy.

Just as Lindsey loved her aunt Linda's celebration of life, so did others. The big, old white Ford van, in which Linda tooled all over town, became a symbol of fellowship and fun.

Whether it was: driving a carload of family members to watch nearly every game her nephew Austin played; hauling members of the church youth group to a work camp; traveling with the Ruby Red Begonia chapter of the Red Hat Society, which she founded; or just making another family ice cream run; you could be sure that there was a lot of laughter in that old van. Except for the fact that it might have been misinterpreted, the tag on the van could well have read: "For a good time, call Linda Miller."

Even the local Roman Catholic nuns shared in the good times. Don't even ask how Linda, a devout Lutheran, knew the nuns of a local teaching order. Linda knew everybody. Soon enough, she had the nuns playing softball with her. One nun, who Linda had dubbed, "Slugger," grieved at the funeral:

"Linda was one of the finest, most thoughtful Christians I have ever met."

"When the nuns invaded your territory," Sister Slugger reminisced in a note to family members, "We were met with hugs, kisses, delicious food and drink and plenty of activities."

"You've got to love a nun called "Slugger." I'm quite sure that nickname came from softball practice and not from a disciplinary practice. For when I met the good sisters at the funeral reception I knew at once that they were "huggers" not "sluggers."

If only I could have had Sister Slugger as my second grade teacher the year my agnostic father decided that a Catholic school was the perfect training ground for a well-behaved, little girl. The second grade would have been a very different experience, had I not have been placed with the short-tempered Sister Ellen Marie, who could never find it in her heart to forgive me for being a Protestant.

Who knows? I might have lived out my later, short-term fantasy of becoming a nun. Not even a teaching nun, I fantasized, but a cloistered, contemplative nun. I imagined myself living in a state of holy grace, serenely tending the beautiful monastery gardens.

The drawback to this fantasy, I later realized, was that the nuns do not hang around the monastery in their spare time. Also, the contemplative nuns have a big thing about "obedience," which has never been my strong suit.

Mother Superior might well have decided to put me in the kitchen. They do things like that, just to keep you used to being obedient. That would have been a disaster. Oh well. The part of taking the vows of silence would have been a deal breaker anyway.

Had she ever gotten wind of my fantasy, Sister Ellen Marie would have been appalled. That first week she managed to convey that it had been difficult enough for her to accept that a "little Protestant" (muttered in a disapproving whisper) had managed to be enrolled at Saint Michael's school. But, that the "little Protestant" had been placed in Sister Ellen Marie's class was a cross almost too heavy for her to bear.

As the "little Protestant," I was none too happy, myself, for I had soon concluded that Sister was my cross to bear. That notion was reinforced every time Sister responded to one of my childish "transgressions" with a sharp yank on the closest ear.

I have often wondered whatever became of Sister Ellen Marie. She might like to tell this story with a slightly different spin. Perhaps she is still around and has become a mellow and kindly Mother Superior.

However, I am not taking any chances. So I have kept the names of Linda's good Sisters anonymous. For, what if Sister Ellen Marie did not change at all and has now become the most superior of Mother Superiors at the nunnery?

"Mother" Ellen Marie would not be happy to hear that today's good teaching nuns are now playing softball and hanging out with Protestants. And I certainly don't want to hear that dear Sister Slugger has had her ears pulled.

Even with the good nuns in her corner, and in the midst of celebrating her life, Linda suffered a major hemorrhagic stroke and died several days later.

"Why the Lord decided to take Linda so suddenly and unexpectedly, we will never know," said Sister Slugger. I guess He just wanted her with Him."

The stroke came without warning one evening as Linda was weeding in the garden, her own calm place. It is quite amazing how frequently the really great people in this world seem to have gardens.

Linda's garden was a country acre with about a hundred bird feeders. Well, actually, about ten. But it seemed like a hundred when all the birds were twittering about. Feeding and watching those birds was, for Linda, a constant source of pleasure and relaxation.

But, that final evening, Linda's enjoyment of the birds was to be short lived. It all happened so fast. One minute, Linda was gardening, alive and vital and the next minute life, as she knew it, was over.

The massive damage to her brain was so traumatic that Linda had no chance for meaningful survival. She never regained consciousness, which was a blessing for Linda, who was able to experience living fully to the end of her days.

Linda's death might not have come so soon, but with her stubborn Pennsylvania German resistance, Linda had refused to comply with her doctor's instructions to continue using medication for her high blood pressure. To her, the side effects of the medication were just not worth it.

It was also quite clear that this was not to be a topic for discussion.

"I don't want to talk about it," Linda informed her family. And that was that.

Still, no one expected her death to come so quickly. We were all more comfortable with denial. It is just too easy to take the lives of people like Linda for granted. Perhaps that is because it is too hard to imagine life without them.

After the fact, her friends wondered if Linda, herself, might have had an inkling that her own life was drawing to a close. For a few days before her death, Linda, who never passed on "sentimental" e-mails, received the following anonymous message, which was making the rounds of the Internet. She immediately sent it to all her friends.

One day a man's wife died, and on that clear, cold morning, in the warmth of their bedroom, the husband was struck with the pain of learning that sometimes there isn't anymore. No more hugs, no more special moments to celebrate together, no more phone calls just to chat, no more "I'll call you right back." Sometimes, what we care about the most gets all used up and goes away, never to return.

Never say good-bye, say......"I love you." So while we have it, it's best we love it, care for it, try not to hurt it, fix it when it's broken, and heal it when it's sick. This is true for marriage.....and old cars, and children with bad report cards, and teenagers with rebellious attitudes, dogs with bad hips, and aging parents and grandparents. We "keep" them because they are worth it, because we are worth it.

Some things we keep —like a best friend who moved away or a class-mate we grew up with. There are just some things that make us happy, no matter what. Life is important, like people we know, who are special and so we keep them close!

And that is pretty much the way that Linda lived her life, knowing that one should live today to the fullest because tomorrow is not promised here on Earth. Perhaps Linda did sense that her own death was nearing. This was a subject that she had occasionally pondered over but did not fear.

"I'm wondering what death will be like," Linda, matter-of-factly, informed her sister-in-law shortly before her stroke. Had I been there I probably would have told her that I was quite sure that, for her, it would be okay. Because she was Linda, so how could it not be okay?

This is not to imply that Linda was some kind of saint. She most certainly was *not* a saint. She was much too stubborn to qualify for sainthood. Had she ever heard herself compared to a saint, Linda would have thrown her head back and given that famous laugh that ended with a little snort.

Anyway, Linda would have hated being a saint. They never got to have all the fun that Linda had. Whoever heard of laughing it up with a saint? Sainthood is probably overrated anyway. Historically, most of the saints ended up rather badly. They were always getting stoned, bloodied up, or burned at the stake.

The significance of Linda's life was not to be found in sainthood, but rather in the well lived sheer ordinariness of it all. I believe that it is in the commonality of our ordinariness that we are all called to be there for each other. And, in doing so, we become the people of peace.

So, it is not really about Saint Peter at the Golden Gate with a list.

But, if there was a list, you can just bet that Linda's name would have been on it.

God holds a special place for peacemakers.

nine

Celebrate Life

*Life isn't about waiting
for the storm to pass......
It's about learning
to dance in the rain!*
—*Anonymous*

Celebrate Life

Occasionally, one of my clients will allude to making an assumption that, unlike them, I live in an eternally pleasure filled, trouble free world.

Oh yes, I live in a little stress-free Eden, surrounded by dancing animals with big, round eyes and a large, perpetually happy family. Every day we all join hands and circle the house singing, "These are a few of my favorite things…."

Well, not all the time.

Who does? But, I am increasingly aware of changing the pattern of my life to focus less on hassles and more on awareness and gratitude for all the good things around me.

From this perspective, every morning is a new day and that itself is cause enough for celebration. Loving and valuing this life, both our own and others, is an early start on the road to peace.

Getting there is not so difficult. Although, as humans we consider ourselves to be the "most evolved" life form on earth, we could all learn a few valuable lessons, just from watching how our dog approaches life: with warmth, caring, forgiveness and sheer pleasure.

If you are dog-less, here are some suggestions gleaned from the internet. One can only assume that the author is a dog, who prefers to remain anonymous.

> *When loved ones come home, always run to greet them.*
> *Never pass up an opportunity to go for a joyride.*
> *Allow the experience of fresh air and the wind in your face to be pure ecstasy.*
> *When it's in your interest, practice obedience.*

Let others know when they have invaded your territory.
Take naps. Run, romp and play daily.
Thrive on attention and let people touch you.
Avoid biting when a simple growl will do.
On warm days stop to lie on your back in the grass.
On hot days, drink lots of water and lie under a shady tree.

When you're happy, dance around and wag your entire body.
No matter how often you are scolded, don't buy into the guilt thing
and pout.....run right back and make friends.

Delight in the simple joy of a long walk.
Eat with gusto and enthusiasm. Stop when you have had enough.
Be loyal. Never pretend to be something you're not.
If someone is having a bad day, be silent, sit close by And nuzzle
them gently.

Whether it is a good day or a bad day, our Lulu has that nuzzle part down pat. And, as a one hundred pound Doberman, that is a lot of nuzzle. Our family's dogs are always rescue adoptees. So, early in their days with us, friends often ask, "Why do your dogs always start out so neurotic?"

They would not be asking that question if they had any idea of the levels of cruelty that some humans are capable of inflicting on helpless animals, which is why we always try to give one of these victims a second chance at having the life they deserve.

The real miracle is that the forgiving nature of dogs allows them, when given enough time and caring, to open up to trust and loving again. Pythagoras was right: "Animals share with us the privilege of having a soul." There is nothing quite like the thrill of watching a formerly, withdrawn, nervous dog go bounding through the yard, tail wagging and joyously celebrating life.

Unlike so many rescue dogs, our Lulu was never abused. On the contrary, she started life as the adored puppy of a young bachelor. As she grew up, Lulu shared his home, his bed, his food and his life. Then, abruptly, everything changed.

The bachelor fell in love with another female. But, this one was to become his wife. The young woman was no fan of dogs. Soon, she made that fact abundantly clear. Their apartment was not big enough for two females.

"It's her or me," was the ultimatum. Sadly, the bachelor transferred the ownership of his beloved Lulu to a rescue group. It is hard to imagine how anyone could ask the person they loved to give up a pet that they had raised and loved so dearly. Personally, I think that the man gave up the wrong bitch.

His loss became our joy, as Lulu grew to understand that ours was to be her forever home and that she would never again be abandoned. But, even now, several years later, she has to make sure and continues to follow us from room to room.

We should have named her "Velcro," for like Rachel in the Bible, Lulu's mantra has become: "Wither thou goest, I will go." And, although she loves us both, if Lulu had to choose, her first choice would always be Stan, for Lulu is a daddy's girl.

Like the "mindful" existence of most dogs, Lulu lives in the eternal present. Yesterday is over and forgotten and tomorrow is not yet on her radar screen. Each day, she is filled anew with delight when her harness and leash appear, as if she hadn't just seen them the day before.

Each daily walk becomes the source of another celebration. Never, it seems, will Lulu ever understand why her humans do not appear to value the exquisite experience of stopping to thoroughly sniff the ground, as if every single exotic scent is actually a personalized business card, which has been left by a previous traveler with a message just for her.

For Lulu, doing her own "business" involves some serious contemplation and preparation before the exact spot can be selected. Usually, several sites must be scoped out, tried and then rejected, before the final place is picked for this honor.

Lulu knows that this is clearly an offering of great importance, because her humans always pick it up in a little plastic bag to bring home and save in a big can that is filled with lots of other good smelling things.

To celebrate her contribution, Lulu immediately launches into her famous "poop dance." Leaping into the air, she prances on her hind legs. Then, after dropping onto all fours, she shifts her weight to her front feet and lifts her back legs, waving them high in the air. Only after this ritual, can Lulu return to her walk, strutting proudly with the knowledge that no other dog has ever done anything quite so wonderful.

The joy of life is only dampened on the occasions when Lulu realizes that her humans will be leaving for a meeting and they will be going without her.

"Oh no!, " she is wiped out. This is the end of the world. "Why, why do you have to go?"

"We'll be back soon," we always remind her. But, only after our little drama queen has made sure that we are aware of the depths of her despair, does Lulu settle in comfortably with her bone, knowing full well that we will soon be returning.

No matter how short a time we have been gone our homecoming is always greeted with great delight. Suffused with joy, Lulu dances and wriggles, all the while wagging her stumpy, little tail. Forgotten is her recent despair. Joy has returned as, once again, Lulu is reminded that this is truly her forever home.

Gratitude for that "forever home" has always been a constant with every abused or neglected dog that we have welcomed into our home. The only sad thing about adopting a rescue dog is that they are often older dogs. So, after you fall in love with them and they become family members, they will continue to age. And all too soon, it seems, your good friend will leave you.

When it comes time for your beloved dog to make that last sad journey and cross over the Rainbow Bridge, then all you can do is weep and remember Shakespeare's advice that "it is better to have loved and to have lost, than never to have loved at all." So true. But knowing that does not take away the pain.

That is just how it was with our beautiful, big, black Doberman, who we called "Oboe, the Always Boy." As his name implied, even at age six, Oboe never really grew up. Sadly enough, the "always" part did not really mean forever. But Oboe enjoyed every moment of his happy life as a big, one hundred plus pound baby.

According to Dr. Popa, Oboe's favorite vet, just as Lulu was a "daddy's girl," Oboe was a "mama's boy." So, when it was time to enter the doctor's examination room, Oboe became the ultimate non-compliant patient.

With his head on my lap, Oboe would lean into my chair, roll his eyes and whimper. Finally, when he refused to get on the scale and instead, tried to crawl his entire hundred pounds plus into my lap, the doctor suggested that it might be better if I left the room. The minute the door closed behind me, Oboe, that big fraud, stepped obediently onto the scale and sat patiently through the entire exam.

Some people might even laugh at Oboe for being such a big ham. But his behavior was easier to understand if you remember that he was a rescue dog, whose early life had been one of pain and neglect. He was finally saved when his owner's neighbors reported this case of animal abuse. And so, Oboe was rescued by DAR&E, the Doberman rescue group.

These volunteers are wonderful people whose big hearts can never turn away a needy Doberman, no matter how old, damaged or sick that dog may be. Under their loving care, the dogs are healed and learn to trust again.

Only then, are the dogs ready to be adopted into their new "forever homes." After seeing the before and after pictures of some of these formerly sad, abused dogs, who are now happy and shining with health, I truly believe that heaven holds a special place for people who care for animals.

And that is how Oboe came to bring joy into our lives and to teach us that every day is another day to celebrate just being alive. So that you can better understand this experience, I will share with you, in his own words, the letter that Oboe wrote for the DAR&E memory book.

To all the good people at DAR&E,

Anyone who met me now would never believe that my early life was so sad. But that was before I found my " always home." In the beginning I was so confused after being neglected, rescued and then shuffled around. My "always mom" says that at first, I was suffering from an abandonment depression. But hey, she's a psychotherapist and they talk like that. Anyway, I just want everyone to know that I am such a happy boy now.

My early name was one of those stupid sounding "I'm-a-really-tough-mean-dog kind of name. But that was from the bad old days. Now, my "always name" is "Oboe." It took me awhile to figure that one out, because my " always mom" says, "Who loves you, Baby?" when she hugs me. Sometimes I think that "Baby" might actually be my real name.

Some people might even say that I am a little spoiled—just because my "always dad" will drop everything to take me for long walks in the woods. He even gets up early in the morning to scramble an egg just for me, because he knows that it makes my dry food so much tastier.

I do follow the rules though, even the silly ones, like don't jump up on the couch. I listen really well –most of the time. And that means even for that other silly rule about not jumping up on people just because I'm excited. I know. I know. I'm a really big boy. But when my humans leave I get really sad. So I give them my best guilt trip look, complete with eye roll.

At last I've finally learned that they will always come back. When they do I just get so happy and excited that I can't even stand still. I just shake and wiggle all over. Then, because I can't jump up, I race to the kitchen and run round and round the table. My humans laugh and clap and go "woo—woo—woo" and pat me every time I pass them. Then, when I calm down, I get hugs and kisses. It doesn't get any better than this!

All this and now I've become a therapy dog, too. Sometimes, I get to be part of my "always mom's" psychotherapy sessions. Even though usually my job is just to be sitting there quietly, I know exactly when an unhappy kid needs a warm Dobe head on her lap.

And that's not all I do. I watch over the house like the best guard dog ever. Nothing gets past me. Now when my "always mom" stays up late at night writing another stupid book, she doesn't have to worry anymore, because I stay up with her. And I can scare off prowlers, but good. No one messes with my people.

Everyday is playtime for me. My humans are environmentalists and they just roll their eye when I run through our wooded acre. They call it "habitat" which means that they encourage all kinds of odd creatures to live here.

Well, they can call it "habitat." I just call it "open season" on the chipmunks. Sometimes my "always mom" has to go and spoil it all. She lets me out the door and then right away she starts yelling: "Here he comes. Run for your lives!"

When I finish my hunting games, what I like best is to just lie out in the warm sun and soak up the peace. If you saw me just dozing here, looking all warm and shiny, you would say to yourself, "Oh, what a beautiful, happy dog!" And it's all because some kind rescue people cared enough to protect me when I needed it.

Rudyard Kipling completely understood what it means to have a dog in your life. He could have been speaking about Oboe when he wrote his famous words about the beginning days of "dog" in this world.

"..........When man waked up he said, "What is ' Wild Dog' doing here?" And the woman said, "His name is not 'Wild Dog' any more, but the 'First Friend,' " because he will be our friend for always and always and always."

But Oboe did not get to have always and always and always. One morning after two weeks of vet appointments for what appeared to be Wobbler's Disease, our beloved "Oboe—The Always Boy," woke up paralyzed and was raced to the hospital for emergency surgery.

Suffering from thornacolumbar intervertebral disease, complicated by Von Willebrand syndrome, which caused extensive internal bleeding, Oboe bravely struggled to survive. But, even with the finest medical care, he just couldn't make it.

After three surgeries, the doctors sadly informed us that it was time to let him go. The day we helped Oboe to cross over the Rainbow Bridge was one of the saddest days of my life.

To help us through those final moments, the hospital had prepared a quiet, private grieving room. Oboe was laid on a nest of warm blankets, supported with soft pillows. We gently cradled him and stroked his head as we told him what a good boy he was and how much we loved him.

As we gently said our goodbyes, we tried to focus on the happy memories of his joyful life and the way he had taught us all to remember to let go of the bad stuff in our lives and to joyfully celebrate the good.

Our loving companion to the end, Oboe's last act on this earth was to lick the tears from my face as he lay dying in my arms.

Oboe taught us well. Although we do not race through the garden as he did, we do celebrate life there. And in one garden corner there is a small stone angel commemorating that here was where Oboe once ran and played.

Symbolically, that statue reminds us that Oboe got it right; a garden is for play, as well as for peace. Even Thomas Aquinas, a 13th century theologian and lover of peace recognized the importance of play as preparation for peace:

It is requisite for the
relaxation of the mind that
we make use from time
to time, of playful deeds.

Many of our "playful deeds" have been centered around the good times in the garden, which is more than just a garden. It is also a place that is about family, friends and celebration. Part of the joy of having a garden is the wonderful backdrop it provides for sharing the good times with each other.

Otherwise, just doing garden work with no play would be like owning a hammock and never taking the time to actually lie in it because you are too busy weeding around it.

Summertime at our house has always been festival time. Nothing is too insignificant to celebrate. The word "great" has been used quite liberally. In past years this has included the "Great Petunia Festival" and the "Great Croquet Festival." The latter came complete with everyone in Victorian costume.

The best times were when the cousins from far and near all arrived. There were hugs and greetings and just generally a lot of noise. The old lap pool sparkled and the patio tables were filled with food.

Nearby, the pergola table was carefully covered and crowded with supplies for the latest project du jour. For, after swimming and feasting, it was always time to create a little something special for the children to bring home.

We made necklaces from unity stones, iced cupcakes, painted rocks, decorated bird houses and crafted floral wreathes. The really fun part was just doing it all together. And then, all too soon, the day would be over. With each festival I wanted it to last forever, knowing all the while that nothing ever does.

Now came the time for hugs and goodbyes and "let's do it again soon." The children, too, were sensitive to the poignancy of this moment. One of my fond memories is of Brian and Patrick, contributors of much of the noise and confusion, but now tired and happy, at the close of a long, full day. Seated together on top of the patio railing, they stared up at the stars, oblivious to everyone else.

"Don't you just love coming to Allie and Poppy's," whispered Patrick.

"Yes," echoed Brian, "I just want to re-wind this whole day and run it all over again."

And so do I.

Then, sometimes when you least expect it, the memories of a really great day just come bouncing back. It was like that one fun filled festival afternoon when the girls and I had walked through the garden and talked about butterflies.

Olivia, though only in the early years of grade school, already the family aesthetic, was entranced. It was no surprise when she later became an artist.

A few days later I was delightfully surprised to open my mailbox and find a fat letter from Olivia. Inside the envelope was a carefully crafted, sky blue plaster butterfly; a generous gift from my little niece.

The enclosed letter explained it all:

To Alice

_____

your garden is
*   so pretty!*
*   when I saw*
this in my room I
wanted to give it to
you because you garden is
so pretty. I thot
of you when I saw
it because I know

you like natcher

———————————————

love, Oliva

Olivia, our budding artist, gardener, was right. I do like "natcher"—a lot. And, one way or another, I can generally be found celebrating it.

Sometimes it might just be Stan and me sitting in the gazebo discussing the next presidential elections, or maybe even "the meaning of life," over a gift bottle of Dom Perignon presented by our children, with the added birthday message, "You're too old to have never tasted Dom Perignon."

Or, maybe later in the gazebo as the conversation dies down; just feeling comfortable with the silence and with each other, watching as the sun slowly sinks, basking the garden in a soft amber glow.

The silence is broken only by the twitters and chirps of the birds in the treetops. They are challenging each other with reminders that it is nearing the evening bedtime and "*I* have claimed this branch."

The birds' interactions are probably the avian equivalent of the social vocabulary of a human two-year old. "Mine! Mine!," being the toddler's second favorite word. The first being "No!"

Unlike the two-year olds, the birds say "Mine! Mine!" in a most melodious way that only adds to the tranquility of the waning day.

The next morning the celebration begins all over again. Entering the garden as the day opens, I feel the calm ease into my body as the sun warms my shoulders. It only gets better at the sight of the chipmunks scouring about and the sound of the birds, who have temporarily finished with their territorial battles and are already up and busily singing about a new day.

I can only sit quietly, feeling a small part of the "eternal song of life." Here, for me, is where peace begins. Like the poet, Mary Oliver, I just want to say:

> *Watch now, how I start the day*
> *In happiness, in kindness……*

And that, for me, is what it means to celebrate life.

ten

A Scorpion in Eden

Never travel faster than your
guardian angel can fly.
—Mother Teresa

A Scorpion in Eden

Celebrating life and talking about peace in quiet, serene settings is much easier than actually practicing peace in less optimal settings.

There is an old zen parable which speaks to this dilemma. Henri Nouwen, a Catholic priest and theologian, shared this story in his discussion of compassion.

THE OLD MAN AND THE SCORPION

Once there was a very old man who used to meditate early each morning under a large tree on the banks of the Ganges River in India. One morning, having finished his meditation, the old man opened his eyes and saw a scorpion floating hopelessly in the strong current of the river. As the scorpion was pulled closer to the tree, it got caught in the long tree roots that branched out far into the river. The scorpion struggled frantically to free itself but got more and more entangled in the complex network of the tree roots.

When the old man saw this, he immediately stretched himself onto the extended tree roots and reached out to rescue the drowning scorpion. But as soon as he touched it, the animal jerked and stung him wildly. Instinctively, the man withdrew his hand, but then, after having regained his balance, he once again stretched himself out along the roots to save the agonized scorpion. But every time the old man came within reach, the scorpion stung him so badly with its poisonous tail that his hands became swollen and bloody and his face distorted by pain.

At that moment a passerby saw the old man stretched out on the roots struggling with the scorpion and shouted: "Hey, you stupid old man. What's wrong with you? Only a fool risks his life for the sake of an ugly, useless creature. Don't you know that you may kill yourself to save that ungrateful animal?"

Slowly the old man turned his head, and looking calmly in the stranger's eyes, he said, "Friend, because it is the nature of the scorpion to sting, why should I give up my own nature to save?"

"Why not?" I asked myself.

Why not, indeed? Because it's damn scary. That's why not. But, Nouwen persists, should we give up our compassionate nature, even if it means we may get stung in a sometimes cruel, stinging world?

The story, says Nouwen, "holds out a great challenge to a society in which we are made to believe that mutual struggle dominates the process of human development. It challenges us to show that to embrace is more human than to reject, that to kiss is more human than to bite, to behold is more human than to stare, to be friends more human than to be rivals, to make peace more human than to make war—in short, that compassion is more human than strife."

Nouwen is right. However, I tend to stay away from the biters. But sometimes they find me. Just like in Eden. There is often a snake in the garden. And that is exactly what happened to me when the calls began…..That first call came late on a cold Saturday night. And nothing was ever the same again.

"Too late for telemarketing," I muttered, dragging myself from delicious solitude, a good novel and the warm cocoon of a blanketed couch.

"Hello—"

Silence. The line hummed. Or was that breathing?

"I saw you today," the caller whispered. "You were buying bread at Giant." Sharing that he had followed me, his whispers were warm and strangely intimate, too intimate. It felt as though we were sharing a bed.

"Why are you calling me?" Can that be my voice shaking?

Silence.

"You asked for it," a coarse whisper now. The affection replaced with a cold rage.

What to say? What to say? Mind racing, but unable to mount a coherent response, I silently replaced the receiver. Little did I know that this was only the beginning.

In the months that followed there were more calls, all untraceable. Sometimes the caller pleaded for intimacy. Other times he was angry that I was "rejecting" him. Clearly, this man was operating on the delusional belief that he and I had a relationship. Soon the calls became more menacing.

On one occasion, my husband and I had traded cars and he remained at home, leaving my car alone in the driveway. Soon the phone began to ring. Stan had barely lifted the receiver, when a man's voice began to sing.

"If I can't have you, no one will," the song began. With no desire to hear the remaining verse, Stan hung up. Later, one police officer suggested that we converse with the caller, in an attempt to discover his identity. Another officer insisted that remaining on the line would only encourage the caller.

As a psychotherapist, I had read about delusional disorders. But, *reading* about delusions is not at all like being the object of one. Listening to someone who believes that you should be seriously hurt because you have betrayed a relationship that doesn't exist is a terrifying experience.

Sometimes called erotomania, this delusion of being loved by someone, who may not even be aware of the stalker's existence, is not necessarily based on the victim's age or appearance but rather, on the stalker's need to connect, or even merge, with that person.

For the stalker, this delusional state can persist for years, or until another love object is found. One police officer informed me that he had been on a case where the woman had been stalked for more than 20 years. That was comforting.

The precipitating attraction for a delusional relationship sometimes takes root in a situation where the potential victim is totally unaware that a "relationship" has already been triggered. The common description of the victim is often that she is "a nice, giving person," sometimes older and more professionally established than her stalker.

For the delusional man, the trigger may have been no more than a friendly smile or an occasion where the future victim has offered some small supportive gesture, which she has long since forgotten. But, with that single act, the stalker now believes that he has found a love object.

One close friend suggested that perhaps the reason that I had become a potential victim, was because I continued to remain confident in situations that others would find risky. I, of course, immediately rejected that possibility.

Later, I came to consider that perhaps my friend had a point. For, as she pointed out, I had, at one time, found it perfectly natural to: direct a youth crisis center, located in an apartment building a across from a busy shopping mall, which offered support to anyone who walked in off the street; to "rescue" kids who went into unsafe city streets at night; or just to strike up friendly conversations with people in the local shopping mall. (Although, I did meet a really great yoga teacher that way.)

"You live as if you have a guardian angel always watching over you," said my friend. Actually, that is pretty much what I believed. "If you do the right thing with love, then everything will work out," was my philosophy. I have since discovered that it does not always work out that way. But, I still believe in the love part.

When the harassment first began, I wanted to believe that, in a dysfunctional way, the caller only wanted what we all desire, a loving, caring relationship. Yet, all too soon, I began to realize that, just as it is with scorpions, you simply don't change another person's reality, just because you would like them to fit your expectations. And, when that person's desire gets acted out in a destructive way, compassion can quickly turn into fear.

Little by little, I succumbed to a deep sense of vulnerability, as the man we dubbed R.C., now began to make more phone calls, followed by nocturnal visits to our enclosed back garden, leaving cigarette butts and less attractive mementos.

I had always perceived myself as a powerful woman, in control of my own life. As R.C.'s presence continued to intrude into my life, that power was eroding. Now, I only felt weak and helpless.

"Get a gun," suggested a police officer, after responding to several cases of vandalism, including an aborted attempt to pick the lock on our front door.

"I can't get a gun. I just don't believe in killing," I protested piously. Perhaps just a little too piously because, growing deep inside, there was now a very strong part of me that was beginning to feel that if someone was going to get hurt, I would prefer that it was R.C rather than me.

"If you do shoot him, don't do it on the street. Make sure that he is already on your property," added the police officer, as if I had not just refused to get a gun.

The following week, we discovered more property damage and the gift of a large camouflage t-shirt draped over a patio chair. This was no small feat because the patio is surrounded by a locked, six-foot tall, stockade fence.

"We told you," chided the returning officer. "The next time we might not be able to get here soon enough. You need to protect yourself. Get a gun!"

I have only gratitude for the police of this county, who have always been so supportive and so responsive to our calls. But, the dilemma of bearing arms continued to haunt me. When does fear justify violence? How do I value another's humanity, and still protect my own?

But, pacifism can be shattered by fear, I discovered, as I continued with my effort to remain peaceful in what, for me, had now become a non-peaceful world. Most of us, in this country, take our safety for granted – until we lose it.

My formerly casual life stance was replaced with a heightened startle response. A sharp knock on our door, or a strange noise, now triggered a startle response.

"Oh no! Is that him? What do I do?" was now my panicked reaction, as fear replaced confidence. Hyper vigilance became my constant companion. Coming home late at night now meant remembering the police warnings. "Do not get out of your car without checking the surrounding area."

Once inside the house, my anxiety level rose as soon as the lights were turned off for the night. Every creak inside the house and every thump outside, now took on a potentially sinister meaning. A good night's sleep soon became only a memory. Although, I still chose not to own a gun, I now had a greater understanding of those who felt the need to be armed.

I had yet to resolve this dilemma when, alone in the house, one sunny afternoon, the doorbell rang. I opened the door, only to spot, parked in our secluded, tree-lined driveway, a plain, unmarked, windowless van.

"Oh my God!" I gasped, for there on my doorstep stood a husky young man wearing a lot of hair, a white t-shirt and camouflage pants, which exactly matched the shirt R.C. had previously left in our garden.

"No," I screamed. Then something interesting happened. All the fear and trembling within me coalesced into an avenging angel. The rage was so powerful that I could only grab the doorframe and, taking advantage of all my yoga training, I reared back and aimed a powerful kick, straight to his groin.

"Help! Stop, lady! I'm the electrician," screeched the terrified man, leaping to the side and grabbing his crotch. Fortunately, I was able to pull back in time, so the electrician did not have to lose the possibility of any future progeny.

After the necessary apologies, I rejoiced in the knowledge that I *could* protect myself. I knew then, in one of the defining moments of my life, that I would never feel powerless again.

And I still don't have a gun.

This episode does not end with a completely satisfying conclusion, for the mystery of R.C. has never been resolved. However, the police do have a possible candidate. From time-to-time a new threat emerges. But, I no longer live in fear.

I can take care of myself; with a little help from the police, a state-of-the-art security system and a very large Doberman, who does not take kindly to intruders. She is soon to be joined by a hefty, big brother. Although, it probably would not be appropriate to call them "Smith and Wesson," two Dobermans will substitute nicely for a gun.

So, I still get to call myself a pacifist. Well, mostly.

eleven

God's Broken Children

*We can let the
circumstances of our
lives harden us so
that we become increasingly
resentful and afraid, or
we can let them soften us
and make us kinder.
You always have the choice.*

—Dalai Lama

God's Broken Children

Given the choice to be hardened by life's pains, or to be kind, I really try to choose kindness. But, sometimes when others, who are acting on their own pain and brokenness, become threatening or violent, then remaining kind is not so easy.

I know in my heart that in, some ways and to different degrees, we need to remember that we are all God's broken children. It is, as my pastor, Roy Howard, recently preached so eloquently:

> *I think a symbol of the Church fulfills its purpose best when it actually connects to what is real. And what is more real than the fact that we are not perfect people? Yes, you are God's beloved, but you are also a person who is......... how shall I put it?.......slightly cracked. It may be so slight that you hardly notice and probably others don't notice about you.*
>
> *On the other hand, some of us have cracks that are obvious to anyone who spends even a passing moment with us. Let's just say my family is well aware that I am cracked. And, sorry to put it this way; so are you.*
>
> *Augustine thought the cracks come with the human condition and are embedded in being mortal. He echoes what Saint Paul says so honestly about his struggles to be faithful: "I do not understand my own actions.....The good that I wish to do, I don't do and the evil that I do not want to do, is what I do."*
>
> *Henri Nouwen, of blessed memory, speaks of "The Wounded Healer." 'Our wounds once healed, remain with us; something like the permanent scars that remind you of the time you scraped your knees or broke your heart. From those healed wounds we are capable of joining in empathy with others whose wounds remain places of pain.'*

Finding Peace In Our Thyme | 93

This, I believe, is where forgiveness enters our lives. Even while acting to protect myself, I want to be able to view a man who stalks me, not as an evil person, but as someone, however delusional, who may be suffering from his own isolation and is now acting from a longing for connectedness.

Although, I now wonder, is forgiveness always possible in any situation? I once thought that it was. But, the bullet in my granddaughter's brain changed everything.

Michelle was so young when that bullet ended her life. Sometimes it seems like every day the media reports another story of one more child lost to a violent death. The news moves on, but the scars remain. Murder is never just one death. The pain ripples through a family and a community.

Michelle lived her brief 17 years to the fullest; as an honors student, athletic star, tutor, "Best Buddy," and friend to so many. Wild and free, Michelle was filled with life and spirit.

Determined to reach her goal of becoming a soldier and psychologist, Michelle fell for the siren song of an Army recruiter, who promised her a college education, followed by a graduate degree, which would enable her dream of supporting the wounded warriors. Instead, she became one.

Michelle, who was so full of heart, was long on trust and short on experience. She was just too vulnerable. When her 31-year old Army Sergeant recruiter, became her superior officer and then seduced her, she mistook it for love.

So, when the Sergeant texted her one Sunday night to say that he was feeling suicidal, Michelle never questioned it. Trustingly, she dashed off into that dark night, never doubting that she could save him.

Instead, Michelle was unable even to save herself. After her father drove all night, vainly trying to locate his daughter, Michelle was discovered the next morning inside the Sergeant's disordered apartment. Her lifeless body had suffered a broken neck and a bullet-shattered brain. Only after he had destroyed her, did the Sergeant put a bullet in his own brain.

All That Bright Light: a Soul Uncovered, has plumbed the depths of that story. I cannot bear to go over it again. I can only say that I have struggled to forgive all those who participated in the events that led to Michelle's death and can only hope that in, either participating, or looking the other way, they did not grasp the tragic ending that was the outcome of their unwillingness to act.

Yes, I do wish that those unwitting participants were now feeling some remorse. Michelle deserves that. But, either way, I do not wish to harbor hatred.

But, what does a "mostly" pacifist therapist say to the 31-year old man who brutally murdered the 17-year old girl who came to save him?

"Oh, I have finally read some of the earlier text messages that you sent to Michelle, in which you bemoaned your pain and shared that: "I destroy everything I care about."

"I feel your pain," was not my initial response. "No, I want to scream. "I don't feel your pain. My own pain is just too great. Why didn't you just kill yourself and be done with it?"

I am not proud of this.

To those kind people who wish to comfort a bereaved survivor, let me offer a suggestion. Show them that you care, hug them, cry with them, but NEVER say, "I feel your pain."

In the early days following Michelle's death, I kept hearing sympathizers attempting to comfort me with echoes of, "I feel your pain." That is so not comforting. I just wanted to scream at them.

"No, you don't feel my pain…..have you ever dreamt, or even imagined, a beloved child, struggling to remain alive, as her attacker overpowers her? In your worst nightmares, can you see a cold, steel gun muzzle pressed against the vulnerable temple of a young, star athlete, with a broken neck, who is now paralyzed and helpless.

" Have you ever agonized with the question: "Did she know what was happening, or was there just a momentary flash before her head was penetrated and her brain – that beautiful mind – was turned into mush?"

No, you don't know my pain and, hopefully, you never will. In healing, I can only hope that, in some small way, I can play a part in saving someone else's child.

Only now, do I have a sense of the hatred that fuels wars. I am beginning to understand a little about the survivors of violence. Some come through with a desire to change their destiny and be a part of changing their world. Others survive with no sense of peace and live in a broken world where their hatred only produces more hatred.

In my darkest moments, I remain inspired by the words of one of my heroes, Martin Luther King, Jr., who reminds me that I want to be one of the people of the light;

> *Darkness cannot drive out darkness,*
> *only light can do that.*
> *Hate cannot drive out hate,*
> *only love can do that..........*
>
> *......I have decided to stick with love.*
> *Hate is too great a burden to bear.*

Sometimes in life, I have discovered, you just have to learn when to let go. There is an old Buddhist tale that speaks to this.

> *It is the story of a young woman's sadness when her baby dies. In her grief, she is unable to accept the death of her child. So, in desperation, she goes to her doctor and pleads for medication. But the doctor knows that there is nothing he can prescribe that will cure this pain.*
>
> *Instead, the doctor sends the young woman to the Buddha.*
>
> *When he hears her story, the Buddha tells the young woman to go out into the community and bring back five white mustard seeds. But, insists the Buddha, the seeds must come from a family where no one has suffered a loss.*
>
> *The grieving woman goes from door-to-door, explaining at each home that she needs five white mustard seeds to use as a medicine for her pain. Most of the families offer to give her the mustard seeds. But every time the woman asks the family if they have lost someone close to them, the answer is always "yes." Eventually, the woman returns to the Buddha.*
>
> *"Have you brought me the mustard seeds?" asks the Buddha.*
>
> *"No," answers the young woman, "but now I understand that there is no family who has not lost someone they love, and I have laid my child to rest."*

Most people who experience pain in their brokenness pose no threat to anyone but themselves. But, there are those who, in their own pain and brokenness, turn to violence.

Increasingly, with the easy access to weapons, these potentially violent people have become a serious threat to the rights of the innocent.

We are blessed to live in a free country with a constitution that respects the rights of every individual. A privilege that we should never take for granted, for not everyone has experienced these rights. Over the years, brave people have fought and died to preserve these freedoms.

This same democracy also carries the seeds of its own destruction. The very freedoms that we enjoy under our constitution are too often used and abused by those whose very deeds undermine the integrity of that constitution.

I support the Second Amendment, which protects our citizen's rights to bear arms. But, the Second Amendment was written by men who had never dreamed of assault rifles and weapons of terrorism.

Now, the NRA uses that Amendment to justify the purchase of guns and assault weapons online and in gun stores and shows. In some states, citizens are allowed to carry concealed weapons and to openly tote assault rifles.

In too many cases it appears that no one is checking on the mental health or past criminal records of the purchasers of those weapons because, say the sellers, "Under the Second Amendment it is the right of every citizen to bear arms."

Have we forgotten that as citizens of America, we also have the right to pursue "life, liberty and the pursuit of happiness?" Hard to do that when you're dead.

One of the most insensitive responses to the issue of gun murders came from Dr. Ben Carson, a respected neurosurgeon, when he was a Republican presidential candidate. He stated that he had never seen a body with bullet holes that was more devastating than "taking the right to bear arms away." I hope that Dr. Carson never has to look at the shot-up body of someone he loves.

Either way, Dr. Carson has missed the point. Most gun control supporters, like myself, are not suggesting that we change the Second

Amendment. We only want to keep weapons away from those violent, criminal or unstable people, who pose a risk to others. Dr. Carson can rest assured. No one is about to take away his gun.

I wonder if Dr. Carson, whose profession is healing, would be receptive to the message of a concerned group called "Heeding God's Call to End Gun Violence." Several times a year this group operates in a different church location and presents a silent message to passersby that every year large numbers of people in their metropolitan and suburban areas are continuing to die from gunshot wounds.

In a quiet ceremony called the Memorial to the Lost, white crosses are pounded into the church lawn. Each cross is covered with a t-shirt bearing the name and age of a gunshot victim who was killed in the previous year.

Victims have ranged in age, from two to seventy-plus. Each shirt is a silent testimony to another death and another family's loss. I will never forget when one of those shirts had read: "Michelle Miller, age 17.

The Memorial is not intended to be a protest about the Second Amendment. It is a wake-up call to bring attention to the hundreds of lives lost every year to the deliberate, or careless, handling of lethal weapons. The plain, small sign in front of the shirts reads: "Stop – Read—Pray—Remember."

Moved by the t-shirts bearing the names of those as young as two and three years of age, Reverend Laura Martin of Rock Spring United Church in Arlington, Virginia, wrote:

A MEMORIAL TO THE LOST

Consider the lilies of the field.
Consider the way they do not
labor or spin —
as they no longer live.
Consider the lilies—
Girl, age 3,
Boy, age 2—
Stilled by bullets.
Consider the way that
Violence showed up

Without a permit
Or background check.
Consider the way
Their right to live
Ended with
A bullet small enough
To be held in their
Hands.

Consider the way we
Sit among the flowers
And grieve.
Consider the way we
Will act for the lilies
yet to bloom.

If you want to see brokenness, just check on any city park bench, beneath bridges or on heating grates in the winter. These are our own forgotten, homeless people. It is to America's shame that some of these men are vets. They, who gave so much, have gotten back so little.

The saddest of these people are the Viet Nam vets. Older now, they didn't even get to be called "heroes," like the vets of the more "popular" wars.

I wonder if anyone ever comes back from the horror of war and manages to remain completely unbroken. America supposedly "won" the Viet Nam war. But, the devastation of the broken lives of many of those who returned, presents a powerful argument for waging peace.

My friend, Smitty, was one of those Viet Nam survivors. He returned bruised, but not broken. Never homeless, Smitty was professionally and outwardly successful, but he never forgot the painful memories of his tour in Viet Nam.

Years later, Smitty still remembered a night on patrol duty when he shot and killed a young Viet Cong sniper, who was poised to attack.

Riddled with guilt, Smitty returned to the same patrol area the next day. Soon, he spotted a young, Viet Cong soldier, who, like Smitty, was also crawling stealthily on patrol.

Calling out to the other soldier, Smitty stood up and with his raised, outstretched arms forming a target, shouted, "Shoot me." The other soldier fired. However, his shot missed wildly.

"You missed me. Try again!" yelled Smitty, maintaining his target pose. Again, the man missed. After the soldier's third failed try, Smitty cursed and walked off.

Hearing that story, I could see two young men who, in another scenario, might have been friends, wondering why they were supposed to be killing each other. Perhaps, they might well have been open to the words of the Dalai Lama:

> *Every single being, even those who are hostile to us, is just as afraid of suffering as we are, and seeks happiness in the same way we do. Every person has the same right to be happy and not to suffer. So let's take care of others whole heartedly, of both our friends and our enemies. This is the basis for true compassion.*

The world can break us all in different ways. For Smitty, the suffering did not end with the Viet Nam war. He returned home to find that the younger brother he had been longing to see again, had become heavily drug addicted. Unable to help his brother, Smitty was now engaged in another war that he could not win.

Unable to "save" his brother who, as expected, died of a heroin overdose, Smitty channeled his grief into a lifelong quest to save other young lives from the self-destruction of drug abuse. This, also, proved to be a war that was never completely "won." But, during his career, Smitty touched a lot of lives, and he let the cracks of light into some very dark places.

When I first met Smitty we were colleagues at a youth residential treatment program. He loved those kids and they adored him. For the boys, he became a powerful role model—a strong, young man, who did not think that drugs were cool.

Instead, he involved them in a Venture Program, where they learned to get new highs by climbing mountains, hiking, kayaking and exploring caves. Smitty laughed at my description of him as a peace maker. But, he was, indeed, for he taught those boys, some of whom had the potential for violence, that there was another way to resolve problems. From Smitty, they learned to explore their own painful feelings instead of acting on them.

The Catholic priest and theologian, Henri Nouwen, would have viewed Smitty's life as an embodiment of his own words:

> *Nobody escapes being wounded. We are all wounded people, whether physically, emotionally, mentally or spiritually. The main question is not "How can we hide our wounds?" so we don't have to be embarrassed, but "How can we put our woundedness in the service of others?" When our wounds cease to be a source of shame, and become a source of healing," we have become wounded healers.*

In later years, as psychotherapists and writers, Smitty and I shared and critiqued each other's words. Frequently, we argued. Sometimes that was enriching and other times we each just went ahead and wrote what we'd planned to all along.

Smitty had been working on the story of a youth treatment program and his dream of making a dent in the world of drug abuse. This was to have been his opus.

When I shared my book *On Becoming a Swan*, Smitty responded: "You already are one and I am sending you a reminder." The following week a small package arrived from across the country. Inside, nestled a tiny, antique crystal swan with silver wings. Sitting on my desk, that little swan is a constant reminder of friendship and support.

Smitty, who presented as so tough, was, as I liked to remind him, a contemporary Don Quixote, tilter at windmills.

Although, he still bore the lasting scars of Viet Nam, Smitty never lost his belief that he could change the world. And always, he wanted to rescue youth from what he saw as the complete devastation of drugs.

Artist, sculptor, and friend to many members of a local ballet troupe, Smitty could openly speak of his own brokenness and still retain his sensitivity to others. A gentle "tough guy," he brought beauty into his life and touched the lives of many of these dancers by seeing the "dulcinea" in each of them.

Smitty would never consider himself to be a pacifist, but he did the things that foster peace. As a professed agnostic, he would have smiled at my suggestion that Mother Teresa could have been speaking of him when she said:

> *I'm not sure exactly what Heaven will be like, but I know that when we die and it comes time for God to judge us, he will not ask, "How many good things have you done in your life?" Rather, He will ask, "How much love did you put into what you did?"*

So, I was not prepared last year, when I received the news that Smitty had been killed in a terrible car accident. Age 67 is much too young to die. Not when you have so much left to do in your life.

In the last days of his life, the biggest "windmill" that Smitty fought was the underworld of drug dealers who preyed on the young. Fearlessly, he searched out the local dealers and exposed them to the community and to law enforcement. Shortly before his death, Smitty even posted a huge sign in front of a local den with the words "crack house," emblazoned in large red letters.

If I had gotten to say goodbye, I would have said: "Oh Smitty, you took too many risks, brave warrior. But, for you, the sense of fear was always outweighed by your sense of mission."

Goodbye, my dear friend. May you rest in peace. You are too soon gone from this world. But you have left your mark on so many. You used your brokenness to heal others and to add light to this world. The last words of Leonard Cohen's *Anthem* could have been written for you:

> *There is a crack, a crack in everything*
> *That is how the light gets in.*

twelve

Us and Them

If we have no peace
it is because we have
forgotten that we belong
to each other.
—Mother Teresa

Us and Them

The Eve of Destruction, for many of us, arrived on November 8, 2016. Most Americans, whether Democrat or Republican, felt that if the other party won, it would mean a devastating crisis for our country.

In those painful days before and after the election, the divisive feelings of "us" and "them" were separating families and friends.

I awoke to despair on November 9. Based on the campaign rhetoric of our now President-elect, I feared how he would implement his proposed plan to "Make America Great Again."

This is a sad day in history, I thought, if we now become a country ruled by rich, old white men, who have forgotten that, except for the Native Americans, we are a nation of immigrants.

Some of these would-be rulers are also men: who are openly misogynist, racist and anti-Semitic; who think that climate control is a myth; who willingly allow our land and water to be polluted by corporations who are mainly interested in the prospect of immediate profit; who do not believe that women should have control over their own bodies; who appear to be insensitive to the needs of their fellow man and who, by condoning these behaviors, have normalized evil.

A number of my friends are people whom I respect for their decency and integrity, are also people who chose to vote for a Republican president. I cannot comprehend the choice they made, but I know that they are kind, intelligent people. They would probably say the same about me.

If the new administration continues in the direction that I fear, I do not believe that my friends will support that. In the meantime, I am not going to let our relationships deteriorate into a state of "us" and "them."

Today's situation is hardly a new phenomenon. Throughout history, peace has eluded mankind with the use of those two simple, little words: "us" and "them." Neighbors, communities and families have erected barriers and sometimes, even fought battles over the all too often minor differences between "us" and "them."

Like everyone else, I have always found it to be more fun to be "us," rather than to be "them." More recently, I have experienced a microcosm of that phenomenon in my own neighborhood. Being a writer and a psychotherapist did not deter me from misinterpreting that experience.

It is hard to believe how much time I wasted by viewing myself as an invisible woman. It wasn't always like that. When we first moved into the neighborhood it had a quiet, suburban, almost rural feeling. But, over the years, with the nearby building of a large Orthodox Jewish Synagogue, I gradually became almost the lone Christian in what has morphed into a large Orthodox Jewish community.

Often, I used to watch from the sidelines as my neighbors walked down the street chattering together in small groups. But, they never seemed to see me. Enviously, I watched, wishing that I, too, could be a part of the community, chatting together as we walked. It was not to happen.

Although I had lived in this neighborhood before they arrived, I was now the outsider. Never was this more obvious than when on an occasional morning walk I would encounter a small group of women and offer a hopeful "Good morning."

Silence reigned. Everyone looked right through me. I had become invisible. I wondered, is it still hostility if no one sees you? Only rarely, one of these women would acknowledge my presence and then it was by staring at me as if I was something stuck to the bottom of her shoe.

Although I strove to maintain a Zen-like stance, accepting without emotion that "it is what it is," sometimes that just didn't work. Then I would get in touch with some hostility of my own. That's the way it was one sunny morning when I walked along the narrow asphalt path en route to the local shopping center and my daily Starbucks fix.

Once again, I faced a duo of stroller pushing mothers, who regularly proclaimed my invisibility be refusing to drop into a single file line, so that we could all remain on the path as we passed each other.

Instead, I was faced with the decision to either leap off the side of the path onto the hilly, uneven ground – or be mowed down.

"Enough," I decided that morning when accosted by the usual stroller group. "Good morning!" I chirped once again. But, this time I was beginning to understand how Rosa Parks must have felt when she decided that she was no longer willing to ride in the back of the bus.

Refusing to leap of the path yet again, I stood motionless, refusing to budge. Fearing that I was about to be mowed down, I silently mouthed my mantra: "I am a rock. I am a rock." Then, "Hallelujah!" At the last minute the Red Sea parted. But still, with eyes averted, they never "saw" me.

"Oh, don't take it so seriously," a suggested a friend. "They don't hate you. You're just not an MOT." For the unenlightened, that means "member of the tribe."

Then I remembered having read a newspaper article in which one member of the community had expressed the opinion that: "We just want to live in a neighborhood with each other and non-Jews should live elsewhere."

Inwardly, I wanted to respond that this had been my community and I was happy to welcome you. But, once here, you decided that it was now your community and you would prefer that I not be here. This sentiment, I suspected, might sound familiar to the Native Americans.

If a Christian was quoted making a similar statement in a newspaper article would they be considered anti-Semitic? I wondered. So does that make the Jewish writer anti- non-Semitic? Why does it have to matter so much? We share the same God. In the areas of faith our common bonds are so much stronger than our differences.

Soon after that experience, at a neighborhood zoning meeting, one of the Orthodox women commented to a friend, "thirty years ago we would not even have been allowed to live in this neighborhood."

That, I am ashamed to say, is a sad echo of the anti-Semitic, racist minority, who all too often, under the cover of Christianity, set up neighborhood covenants which excluded Jews and people of color.

This was in the same shameful era when, in the South, there were cowardly, white men in white robes and pointy hats who burned crosses and called themselves Christians. Sadly, those haters have re-emerged from the shadows, believing that their evil will now be tolerated.

It was in that same period that, as the leader of a Christian youth group, I marched and canvased door-to-door with fair housing petitions. Sadly enough, one member of our youth group was run off the property of an irate, shotgun wielding homeowner, who threatened to kill him if he ever returned.

The teenagers had their first experience of violent bigotry that day. More powerful than any textbook lesson, were the words and actions of hatred that were hurled at them. Fortunately, there were also those homeowners who gladly signed their support of fair housing.

That day proved to be an unexpected growth experience for all of us. Witnessing the hostile behavior of the few bigoted homeowners, led to a youth group meeting, which focused on the subject of "white Christian privilege."

In time, we came to the painful conclusion that as long as we looked the other way and continued to take advantage of this unearned position, we were all a part of the problem.

This growth experience was not universally embraced by many of the church members, who preferred that we pray about these "problems," rather than actually act on them.

The ensuing uproar from those members, coupled with the feelings about our less than popular, inner city youth ministry, contributed to our departure from that church.

Spearheading our departure was the minister, who no longer wanted us as a member of his tribe. He suggested that we would probably be happier in another church. He was right. We were.

Leaving that church was a small price to pay for trying to live what we believed. And, as many clergy persons can attest, trying to follow the actual message of the Bible can occasionally land you in deep trouble with your own church. Fortunately, this was no longer true when we found our safe harbor with Saint Mark Presbyterian Church, where we plan to remain forever.

Desmond Tutu responded to the sad separation between people of faith with his own simple belief that pretty much says it all:

> *I give great thanks to God that he created a Dalai Lama.*
> *Do you really think, as some have argued, that God will be saying,*
> *"You know, that guy, the Dalai Lama is not so bad.*

What a pity he's not a Christian?" I don't think that is the case, because, you see, God is not a Christian."

And, he might well have added, His son was a Jew.

In one of life's little ironies, we now live in another of the communities, where, years ago, we had canvased for fair housing. So when we later moved to and became established in this community, it was difficult to realize that I was not about to become high on the welcome list.

I am reminded of a long ago conversation with a friend who was the newly arrived and lone person of color in a white neighborhood.

"Finally, things are changing," I commented, meaning that she was now a part of the community.

"No," she smiled, wryly, "I just live in the community. I am not apart of it." I, in my ignorance, of course, protested.

"Alice," she rebuked me "you are white. You wouldn't know."

Well, I thought years later, *Now* I know.

Anyway, that is what I once thought. But sometimes just when you think that you know something, you find out that you really don't know at all. This is not a new experience for me.

As any psychotherapist can tell you, when people are ignored they feel rejected. Clearly, I was no exception. It was those feelings, which prompted me to write an article titled *Now I Know*, which, in essence, bemoaned my sadness when the world becomes "us" and "them." This is especially true if you happen to be "them."

Then, serendipitously, things began to shift. As our environmental consciousness increased, my husband, Stan and I began to value lawns less and habitat more. Ultimately, we began the lengthy process of tearing up the front lawn and replacing the grass with beautiful trees, shrubs and wildflowers to create a natural habitat garden.

Soon, as our neighbors walked past our house on the way to Synagogue, many of them stopped to admire the beauty of the emerging garden and to exchange a friendly word. Gradually, we began to experience ourselves as welcomed neighbors. Once again, the garden had worked its magic.

It all came together for me when I shared my *Now I Know* article with my neighbor Rikki, an Orthodox Jew. Not only did she suggest that I show the article to her Rabbi, she also responded with complete surprise that I had expressed a longing to be a part of the community.

"I never knew that you felt that way," said Rikki. As we talked, I began to view my experiences a bit differently.

"In America," Rikki reminded me, "outside of the major cities, we live in a mostly Christian world that has not always welcomed Orthodox Jews. So sometimes the silence and distance that you experience from the Jewish community may reflect the distancing and rejection that we have experienced from Christians."

Until then, it had never occurred to me that my neighbors might have perceived me as potentially hostile.

I was reminded that, prior to the settlement of Israel, the Jews survived for three thousand years without a homeland. They have been bound together by the Torah, which provided them with a code of laws.

When the Jews left the Holy Land and dispersed to gentile nations, they strove to create a diaspora where they could continue to observe the laws and honor the Torah. So this is what community means to them.

And there you have it again, the lack of understanding that separates the world into "us" and "them." When, in reality, the world is, as a friend of mine recently reminded me, "just us and the rest of us."

Now I know. And what better description of my former dilemma than the paraphrase of the Serenity Prayer, which was posted anonymously on the Internet:

> *God grant me the serenity to accept*
> *the people I cannot change.*
> *the courage to change the one I can,*
> *and the wisdom to know that it is me.*

thirteen

A Thyme to Heal

Pain is inevitable
Suffering is optional.
—Zen saying

A Thyme to Heal

Sometimes in life, pain *is* inevitable. The suffering, or at least the degree of suffering, can be optional. Recently, I have found this to be all too true, as I experienced my own reasons to be aware of the mind, body and spirit connections.

I have always taken pride in being a strong woman, so after several years of toughing it out, as my hip continued to deteriorate, I did a pretty good job of denial. But, as the pain worsened, I found that my gait had steadily moved from uncomfortable limping to full-blown lurching.

If I worked hard enough at strengthening my core and back muscles, I reasoned, I could take the stress off my hip. I have always preferred to think of my back as having a naturally curly spine, as opposed to the medical term, scoliosis. I figured, contrary to all medical advice, that I could change this. Physical therapy helped, but not enough to fight nature.

As the pain increased, I eventually lurched into the orthopedist's office. He was not impressed with my naturally curly spine theory. Instead, he suggested that this was a crippling condition. This was not what I wanted to hear. So our continuing dialogue went downhill fast.

"I'm a hipple, not a cripple," I pointed out. He was not amused.

"You need a hip replacement," he insisted.

"A hip replacement could further damage a hip with osteoporosis," I argued. Then the doctor had to go and point out that only one of us had gone to medical school, and that was not me.

"I know that I can correct this with some more strengthening exercises," I wheedled.

"I'll give you some strong medicine for awhile, but I will need to operate," the doctor insisted. "*This* is what I do."

"Well, I'm not willing to take strong medicine. So, I'll stay with aspirin and go to therapy. *This* is what I do." And that pretty much ended the conversation. Exasperated, the doctor gently edged me to the door and ended with the closing words:

"I'll see you when you can't stand the pain any longer," was his parting shot.

You can just guess how this ends. I always hate it when the doctors are right, especially when they gloat.

I hope he doesn't read this.

I lurched along for a while longer. Eventually, trying to keep up my spirits by playing the "Ham and Legs" game, wore thin. Essentially, the game just involves making up stupid answers when strangers persist with annoying and embarrassing questions:

"Why are you in a wheel chair?"

"Well, gee, it's just so much easier than walking." Other times, the best response is just asking a question of my own:

"What do you mean, 'What's wrong with my leg?' There's nothing wrong with my leg. Why do you ask?'" When that got old, I resorted to making up a different story every time:

"It's an old football injury," or, my favorite, "I fell off the stage at National Theater during the second act of 'Cats.'" Mostly, though, I would have to spoil it all by laughing and explaining that this was just a little temporary problem.

Except that it was not a temporary problem. It was getting worse. "Pain is inevitable," I reminded myself, yet again, "Suffering is optional." Striving to be more zen-like, I tried to focus less on the pain and more on the fact that, at least, I was still vertical.

On the plus side, through all this discomfort, I did learn a lot about the kindness of strangers. The caring that I received from people that I didn't even know, fed my belief that most people, at the core, are basically good.

I had doors held open for me, parcels carried and help with stepping off the curb. One woman, seated near a restaurant window, even left her meal to come outside to help me on the sidewalk.

In restaurants, I ultimately developed a method to walk, unaided, to the rest room. As I passed each table, I tried to unobtrusively hold on the edge of the table for balance. Although, I probably looked like an ape, swinging from one branch to another, I preferred to view this maneuver as evidence of my agility.

One elegant, older lady, seeing my hand clutching the edge of her table, was far more concerned with my wellbeing than with the fact that I was dangerously close to upsetting her veal marsala.

"Are you okay, dear?"

"I'm fine," I lied. "I just walk funny."

"Oh, that's okay, dear," she patted my arm. "We all do something a little funny." I would have hugged her, but then, for sure, I would have fallen over into her veal platter.

Finally, the pain drove me back to the orthopedist. Surely, I thought, by now be will have some new ideas. He did not. Instead, he looked at my x-rays and pointed to a small blob on the screen.

"You're out of time. That mass is a cyst that's eroding your bone." The time to argue was over. Surgery was scheduled for the following week.

Because I suffer greatly from anticipatory pain, the ensuing days were difficult. I prefer to call my anticipatory suffering a projected "low threshold of pain." The medical profession considers that term to be a euphemism for "sissy."

I fantasized every possible bad outcome, including a fractured femur that would render me unable to walk. Ultimately, there was a bad outcome, but it wasn't from my shiny, new hip replacement.

My worst fantasy was that the doctor would mistakenly operate on my good leg. Sure, he might figure that out when he opened the wrong hip. But what if he didn't? So, I took my own precautions.

The surgeon was not pleased when he came to my gurney for a last minute pre-op check, prior to entering the operating room. He rolled back the sheet and spotted my good leg, which now sported a row of band-aids from hip to knee. Each band-aid was adorned with large letters inked in with a felt tip pen.

"This is my good leg. Do NOT touch!" was the spelled out message. The doctor was not amused. However, the nurses thought it was funny.

It is only fair to add that the orthopedist was an excellent surgeon and I would not hesitate to recommend him. The pain was far less than I expected. After I regained complete consciousness in the recovery room, I was feeling relieved and no longer anxious.

As I lay there watching the activity in the room, I had an experience that I hesitate to mention, but, to me, it was too important not to share.

To my left, coming down the hall walkway, I noticed a multitude of tiny, sparkling lights that moved down the hall and stopped at the foot of my bed. The sparkles then settled on the white, cotton blanket at the foot of the bed. It was an awesome experience but not scary, and I was filled with a sense of peace.

I fear that my colleagues will suggest that this was just post anesthesia woo-woo stuff. But, I know better. After a few minutes, the sparkles moved back and went slowly down the length of the room before disappearing. I smiled and wondered if my granddaughter, Michelle, so recently lost to us, had come to lend some comfort.

The operation was a success, but the aftermath was a painful and difficult summer. Soon after discharge, I returned to the hospital with internal bleeding, which was diagnosed as ulcers, bleeding from the long term use of aspirin for the formerly unrelenting hip pain.

The next hospitalization might have been a better experience if the ENT, who was scheduled to do the endoscopy, had had a better attitude. The problems started from the moment I was prepped for the procedure.

When I was wheeled into the large room where the procedure was to be performed, I saw that the room was already filled with a multitude of gurneys, all bearing other patients who were awaiting the same procedure.

While I was left unattended, I noticed a young woman in scrubs, who was watching me from the other side of the room. Seeing me alone, she walked over to my gurney, leaned over and whispered in my ear, "Don't let that doctor touch you. I'll come to your room later." But, I never saw her again.

For the next two hours, I lay on that gurney, motionless and uncomfortable, as I waited for the doctor, who never appeared. When a nurse finally came, it was only to clear the room with the announcement that Doctor X was called to another hospital to perform endoscopy there.

After waiting an additional hour back in my room, my anxiety was replaced with anger. I called the hospital ombudsman with the suggestion that she should be aware that it was extremely poor practice to make a large group of people, some with potentially serious problems, wait while the scheduled doctor had trotted off to another hospital.

In a matter of minutes; the ombudsman, the hospitalist, the ENT head nurse, and the now returned, great doctor, himself, were all at my hospital bed. The irate doctor, with his back to the others, faced me with slitted eyes and mumbled through clenched teeth:

"I-am-sorry-to-have-kept-you-waiting."

"No, you're not," I wanted to say. Instead, with the assembled staff listening, I asked: "How could you leave the hospital with a roomful of scheduled patients waiting for you?"

"That other case was more serious than yours," he snarled, not even acknowledging that there were other patients who were also waiting.

"How would you know?" I queried. "You haven't even seen me. Besides, you are not the only doctor in town. It seems like you are just building your practice by packing in more patients than you have time to handle."

"I-will-see-you-right-now," he muttered, and promptly stomped off.

"Now, I'm afraid to have him working on me," I confided to the remaining staff members. They appeared to agree with me, but insisted that it would be risky for me to delay the procedure. I could only speculate that it would be riskier to be sedated and at his mercy.

"I will go with you," volunteered the head nurse. "I will stay right there through the entire procedure," she promised. "And I will be the one to bring you back to your room."

I will always be grateful to that woman. She represents everything that is powerful and good about nurses. She understood. So did my own private practice doctor, who just happened to be in the hospital at that time. At just the right moment, he popped into my room to reassure me.

"You did a good job," he praised. "You took care of yourself."

So, yet again, I have established that I am not the kind of patient that hospitals look forward to seeing. On the other hand, I am the kind that survives. Usually.

**

Once again home, I lasted less than a week before awakening in the middle of the night with terrible chest and abdominal pain. Even I, realized that I was beyond making any choices about alternatives. Soon, I was in an ambulance, speeding toward the hospital.

"Am I dying?" I asked the EMT, as he fiddled with his monitors.

"You're having an MI," he answered. "A heart attack," he added, in case I hadn't figured that out. That got me relaxed right away.

Nonetheless, the EMT was very comforting and made me feel like I was in good hands. Although, sometimes hospitals aren't always so great, I think that EMTs deserve a boatload of gratitude for the valuable service they perform.

The cardiologist raced into the emergency room and determined that this was not a heart attack, but he was sufficiently concerned with the results of the CAT scan that an emergency surgeon was called in.

At that point, had I been functioning, I would have preferred to first check out the professional reputation of the doctor who would be slicing me open. However, I was in no shape to make that call. So, it was luck of the draw. This proved to be my lucky day and I got a very new, but very good surgeon.

After the fact, I was informed that my intestines had apparently not been too happy about the earlier surgery and decided to get all wrapped around each other. By the time the surgeon got to them, they were choked and turning purple, en route to dying.

The rest is too gory to describe, but the short version is that the surgeon unwrapped all the intestines and massaged life back into them. After opening me again the next day he managed to tuck them all in place and save all the working parts. For this, I will always be grateful. I am only too aware that the alternative would have been quite unpleasant.

Now, the only remaining evidence of my hospital experience, are the long thin scars that trail across my midsection. Although, they are not very obvious, they have forever ruined my chances of becoming a centerfold.

The days following my last surgeries were pretty awful. The one saving grace was having a husband who remained with me day and night. Although, he was supported by family members, it was Stan, whose bed was a foldout chair beside me. And it was Stan, who held my hand, stroked my head and called the nurses when necessary.

The surgeon later informed me that I had been near death. But, I already knew that. It was only the presence of Stan that kept me alive.

I do know now that I will never fear death. For, one night, I was aware that I was dying. There were no tunnels or bright lights or heavenly figures that I have heard other people describe. It was a very calm experience of moving on. I knew that I was dying, but I was not afraid.

But, during that gentle calm, I gradually became aware of Stan beside me. His face was next to mine and I could feel the tears running down his cheeks. In those moments everything began to change and I knew that I could not die and leave him.

When, at last, it became time to leave the hospital, the doctors insisted that I be moved to a rehab facility. In our usual family tradition, we disagreed with the doctors. Stan insisted that he could care for me at home. And that is exactly what he did.

If you have ever been a needy patient, you know that caregivers are the unsung heroes of medical support and recovery. You never realize how many simple things in life you take for granted until you can no longer do them.

Suddenly, it is no longer an option to: go to the bathroom alone, to wash up, to eat, to put on your clothes without help or to go outside without assistance.

In the early days of recovery that level of dependence is scary. I can remember laying in bed, needing to go to the bathroom and desperately yelling for Stan, who was in the rec room watching television and unable to hear me.

When he finally came upstairs to check on me I was dissolved in a puddle of self-pitying tears, wondering when I would ever just be able to get out of bed by myself.

Every day, I struggled through my physical therapy exercises, increasing the reps, so that I could more quickly regain the core body strength I needed to get out of the prison that my bed had become.

Soon after I came home, I tossed the remaining oxycontin pills in the trash. I believe that the reward of pain reduction is not worth the price to be paid for putting strong chemicals in my body.

Toughing it out was a bit rough at first. It helps to understand that a big part of pain control is learning to shift your focus. It is not so much a denial of pain, as a realization that you can choose to turn your awareness elsewhere—for a while.

I practiced deep breathing, imagining that with the long inhale I touched the pain center and then with the following long exhale I was releasing the pain, allowing it to flow out of my body. That helped. Somewhat.

Some painful nights, after I could get out of bed by myself, I would sit at my desk and draw in my adult coloring book. When exhaustion finally took over, I would crawl back into bed, where Stan would awaken from his own sleep to rub my back.

Finally, I could drift into sleep, lulled by my focus on those good feelings of the back rub. The healing peace of the human touch is incredible. And, all the time I was reminding myself of how blessed I was to have Stan, the unsung caregiver, who was constantly sacrificing his own needs to meet mine.

I remember, that as a teenager, I was once advised that: "It is just as easy to love a rich man as to love a poor man." With the benefit of experience, I would ask: Does it count that in college Stan worked in the dormitory dining halls to supplement his tuition, but spent his last graduation silver dollar buying me a cheeseburger? But, that's not really the point. Because, you see, I did marry a rich man.

This time of incapacitation served to remind me, that in addition to all the loving support of my family, I am also rich in friends. The caring support of the church family, who called and visited, offered prayers and brought food, filled me in so many ways.

Recovery was also a time of gratitude for the healing peace of my garden. As this chapter title suggests, the garden provided my thyme to heal. How fortuitous it was, that only the year before my surgeries, we had enlarged our sunroom with the addition of a glassed-in herb room.

From this sanctuary, I could view our woodland garden, feel the warm sun on my head and nurture my little herb plants. It was like ingesting all their energy, just to breathe in the crisp scent of the new young herbs.

Of all the plants, it was the grassy, spicy smell of the thyme that lingered on and filled my senses. Soon, I was filling jugs with fresh water and sprigs of mint, rosemary and thyme. Left in the refrigerator overnight to chill and seep, the resulting beverage was so refreshing and calming, that ever since, I have continued to drink it whenever I need a peaceful pause. So, how fitting it seems, that this book has titled itself, *Finding Peace in Our Thyme.*

After my surgeries had healed, I found that my body was not quite finished with its surprises. As I continued to work in physical therapy, it became increasingly obvious that I now had a serious balance problem.

When the therapy center brought in a balance expert. his first question after examining me was, "Have you ever had a brain concussion?" The answer, of course, was: "Yes, years ago, I was thrown from a horse and struck my head on a rock."

Apparently, as the balance expert explained, just as with wrestlers and football players, people who have had serious concussions early in life, will often have return symptoms many years later. My symptoms, he theorized, were triggered by three surgeries and a considerable amount of anesthesia, all occurring in a short time frame.

"This is not correctible," I was informed. "But, it is adaptable." Since I do not plan to go through life falling over every time I turn my head, or get lightly bumped, I have decided that I will just have to adapt the hell out of it.

With enough "adaptation," I figure, my balance problem will be "corrected." Anyway, that is my theory and I am sticking with it.

Knowing that a fall now could have some serious repercussions, I am highly motivated to learn to walk again without support. Now, in physical therapy, after some initial resistance, I have moved to using a ceiling mounted harness.

The security provided by the harness allows me to begin to let go of a walker as a necessary lifeline. Even as I stumble and flail about, I am learning to re-build balance and stability.

Instead of resisting the harness, I now fantasize that as I move along under the track support on the ceiling, I will soon begin to elevate. Then, I can become airborne like the flying nun, offering support to all those poor grounded people below.

In my dreams, I still dance. Even though my dancing is much like my cello playing; filled with great enthusiasm, but lacking in talent, I love the feeling and I want it back. In the meantime, I have learned to be grateful that I am still vertical.

It is just like that old saying that was my grandmother's response to any complaints:

> *I cried because I had no shoes,*
> until *I met a man who had no feet.*

I can accept this, but only if necessary. Because, deep inside, I believe that I will dance again.

***

Not everyone gets to heal. My friend, Lani, who was less broken than most of us, did not. It was several years ago, that Lani first told me that, although she was a non-smoker, she had just been diagnosed with Stage 4 lung cancer.

I felt an overwhelming sadness that someone so special was getting the message from her doctor that, "We will keep you comfortable." What an ominous message.

I was also aware of another deeply selfish and overwhelming feeling that I just couldn't lose someone else that I love. Although she, herself, was unconscious of the fact, Lani was the person that everyone loved.

I hold in awe the people who sincerely pray, "Thy will be done," and actually mean it. When I hear about the impending death of people like Lani, I just have to turn to God and say, "What were you thinking?" Actually, I know that this is not theologically accurate.

Before the cancer reared its ugly head, Lani and I had once discussed death. We both concurred that we were not afraid to die, but we just weren't ready to go yet.

But, no one gets to make that decision and not everyone gets to heal. Lani did not. She had a few more good years. Years, which she made "good," in spite of all the chemo, tests, weariness and nausea. In her last more difficult months, there was always a loving family there for her.

Near the end of her life, while Lani was in hospice, her daughter, Wendy, made her own "gratitude list," which starred the blessing of having had such a loving mother. Wendy, indeed, is her mother's daughter.

"There is no death," said Chief Seattle, "only a change of worlds." This is all very true but, in leaving this world, Lani left an empty place in many hearts.

At Lani's funeral we sang one of my favorite hymns, *Here I am, Lord*. This would probably be considered to be one of the more compositionally poor hymns, but the lyrics speak to me. "I will go, Lord, if you lead me, I will hold your people in my heart." Whenever I now play that song on the cello, it has simply become *Lani's Song*.

Now, on my own gratitude list, I have chosen to follow Charles Schultz's words to live by, as expressed in the cartoon "Peanuts:" Charlie Brown sadly reminds Snoopy that, "One day we will all die."

"True," Snoopy replies, "but on all the other days we will not."

Finding Peace In Our Thyme | 123

Finding Peace In Our Thyme | 129

fourteen

Love is a Verb

No one is useless in this world,
who lightens the burdens of another.
—*Charles Dickens*

Love is a Verb

"I want my life back," I groused in one of my less positive late summer days, after a difficult bout with the physical limitations following my three surgeries.

As a gardener, I bemoaned the fact that I had "lost the entire summer" during my struggles to heal. Gradually though, I once again came to realize that, actually grace had been staring me in the face the whole time.

I had not lost that summer. I had been given that summer. The support and prayers of family, friends and my church was overwhelming.

If you don't believe in the power of prayer, I can only say that I do. For, as I was being prayed for, I was, according to my surgeon, within a couple hours of dying.

All this caring has been the grace in my life. My family, friends and the Saint Mark people just kept sending messages and cards, and daily, visitors kept arriving with food. That is because they knew that, as often has been said, "Love is a verb."

Stan, my husband, has always known this. Willingly, he put aside many of his life interests to care for me at home. This was a decision he made, even after the hospital staff pushed their recommendation that my care needs could more easily be met in a rehab facility. That was a decision for which I still remain profoundly grateful.

In those early weeks of recovery, I could look out my sunroom windows and see the garden bursting with life and waiting for me. I was filled with gratitude and future plans.

At first, my body was still frail. But, my spirit was not. Soon, my body began to catch up, with a little help from my friends – and my visiting physical therapist.

How can I adequately say, "thank you" to: Stan, my lover, best friend and constant support; my family; all my caring friends here, and even on Facebook; and, of course, my Saint Mark family? I can't. The only answer is to live my life as "love passed on," because love is a verb.

All too well, I already knew this from my earlier experiences after my granddaughter, Michelle, was murdered. It was the hugs that buoyed my spirits, the knowing that I did not walk alone. For me, friendship helps more than any dose of Prozac ever could.

It is these acts of kindness, large and small, that bind us together. This was true some years ago when I ran a crisis center and it is still true today. Many of the people who call help centers and hotlines still present loneliness and isolation as one of their major concerns.

Even being fastened to the umbilical cord of an I-pad or texting on a smart phone cannot provide an opportunity to share or explore one's whole self. Emoticons do not substitute for a real in-depth relationship. This loneliness and lack of connection sometimes propels people into psychotherapy.

Sadly enough, too much of psychotherapy today is now structured to meet the demands of the insurance companies. Never is this more apparent than in the large HMO's, who prefer to reimburse a quick fix of short- term psychotherapy, focused more on pharmacology than "talk therapy."

Anti-depressant medications are a powerful tool for relieving the symptoms of a deep depression. And in many cases, medication provides a necessary support for what may be a chemical imbalance in the brain.

All too often, physicians have been quick to hand out prescriptions for powerful medications, with very little knowledge of their patient's mental condition. Anti-depressants are now almost as easy to come by as a bag of M and M's.

Recently, one friend told me that many of her friends were now on Prozac. "It's really easy to get," she said. "All you have to do is go to your GYN for a regular check up and then tell her that you are feeling sad, you cry a lot and you don't sleep well any more."

The second prescription will be just as easy to come by. The good doctor will schedule a follow-up appointment. In the allotted minutes, her patient can briefly mention how she is feeling and if there are any adverse side effects. Then it's off to the pharmacy with a renewed prescription.

Everybody wins. The patient is relieved. The doctor is paid for the brief session. The pharmacy has sold another prescription and the insurance company has paid as little as possible. Of course, nobody mentions that medical research has yet to develop a pill that provides a cure for loneliness or provides insight and support in dealing with life's problems and stresses.

Psychotherapy can speak to these needs, but talk therapy itself, is only as useful as the client's willingness to participate and the skill and sensitivity of the provider.

Therapists, who are totally limited to a narrow treatment modality, often miss the boat when it comes to recognizing what is actually going on with their client.

To me, it seems that sometimes the more rigid followers of the DSM (the psychiatrist's bible, better known as the Diagnostic and Statistical Manual of Mental Disorders) are far more proficient at diagnosing problems than they are at treating them.

While understanding how one's childhood has shaped the person that they have become, is an invaluable experience, peaceful communities develop when individuals move on beyond just exploring their inner child to search for their role in the larger world.

Social workers, who probably comprise the largest group of mental health providers in America, usually focus, not just on an understanding of that inner child, but work on a life model of practice.

This practice focuses on; understanding and working through life stresses, developing interpersonal skills, and building relationships that go beyond the shallow presentation of self, that is often seen on the internet as a substitute for a meaningful connection.

A life model therapeutic approach steps forward from the more analytic, and often distancing stance of some earlier treatment modalities that consider it productive to maintain a strict "therapeutic" distance from their patients, while pointing out what they perceive to be their patient's dysfunctional behavior.

Never have I seen this distancing, analytic philosophy more clearly than I did one afternoon when, as the director of a youth center, I called a consulting psychiatrist for professional support.

Bill, a young man who had walked into the center, had been highly agitated and upset. As he described how unvalued and worthless he felt, it became increasingly obvious that, in addition to having no support system, he was also deeply depressed and suicidal.

I arranged for an immediate hospitalization in the psychiatric wing of a local hospital. Dr. Sensitive, the psychiatrist I had contacted, spoke briefly with Bill and agreed to meet him at the hospital at four o'clock that afternoon. With that promise, Bill agreed to be admitted to the psych unit.

At 8:30 that evening I stopped by the unit to check on Bill. Alone in his room and with no staff member in sight, he lay on his bed in tears.

"I don't know why I even came here," he cried. "Dr. S. never even showed up."

"I know he'll come," I promised. "I'll wait with you."

"He probably doesn't even care," lamented Bill, pointing out that, once again, it was obvious that he was not of much value to anyone.

It was nearly ten p.m. when Dr. S. finally breezed in. Apparently oblivious to the fact that he was now six hours late for their scheduled appointment, he became quite annoyed that Bill did not appear to be at all grateful to see him.

"You said you were coming at four o'clock," Bill greeted him. "I waited and waited for you. You never even called."

I kept quiet, but personally, I thought that Dr. S. might have apologized for his delay and perhaps an explanation that he had been tied up, might have gone a long way towards validating Bill's feelings.

Instead, Dr. S. responded in the ultimate, distancing analytic mode:

"I am wondering if there were times earlier in your life when you felt that someone had let you down?"

The next day Bill signed himself out of the hospital and disappeared. When Dr. S. heard my concerns that Bill was now alone and vulnerable and we had no way of reaching him, he attempted to console me.

"Well, it wouldn't have worked out anyway. That young man was not sufficiently motivated to be in therapy."

Recently, I was reminded of this little scenario with Dr. S, when I read an anonymous parable of 'The Good Samaritan," posted on the

Internet. It reminded me again of that encounter when Dr. S chose to miss his own contribution to his patient's distress.

> *One day a young man was walking down the street alone when a group of thugs accosted him. He was robbed and brutally beaten.*
>
> *While the young man lay on the ground, unconscious and bleeding profusely, a psychologist just happened to be walking by.*
>
> *Seeing the wounded man, the psychologist ran over to look more closely and cried:*
>
> *"My God! Whoever did this needs help!"*

Fortunately, there are many good therapists out there who more than make up for the not-so-good ones. What a blessing for those in pain who find the right psychotherapist. This is the one who lightens their client's burdens by listening to them and by walking with them, without any judging or intrusive instructions.

Margie Nichols, herself a licensed psychologist, describes the healing power of psychotherapy in her own life. In the *Psychotherapy Networker* article titled, *The Valley of the Shadow*, Margie shares her own dark journey.

She relates the tragic story of losing Jesse, her own young daughter, who suffered an awful death shortly before her tenth birthday. After a series of medical catastrophes following brain surgery, Jesse spent her final three weeks of life in a medically induced coma.

It was a terrible way to die and devastating for her mother. Perhaps only another mother who has lost a child can even begin to understand the depth and devastation of that grief.

For the first couple years following Jesse's death, Margie describes waking up every morning with the same thought:

"I'm still alive? I've really got to drag myself through another day?"

"Suicide was out of the question," she says. "So I went into therapy instead." Her story is a testament to the pain of grief and the healing power of therapy.

> *Now I'm not the easiest person to find a therapy fit for—and not just because I am a therapist. I'm queer, but I'm also a Baby Boomer, lefty, liberal, second-wave feminist, atheist, hippy peacenik. A likely fit*

might've been a feminist woman, or maybe a gay man. Instead, I was drawn to a colleague whom I'd first met as a couples-counseling trainer in a program I'd attended 15 years earlier. Bruce, the therapist I picked, was way at the other end of the Boomer continuum. He was an older, white, straight, Midwestern guy. An ex-Marine. An ex-seminarian. My guess was that he voted Republican.

Bruce was a tall man, thin and kind of severe-looking. He had a calm, level neutral way about him, and at times, with his pale skin, he could look almost ghostly. I'm not saying he was cold, because he wasn't, but he didn't do warm and fuzzy either. He had a poker face and talked in a kind of deadpan way—quiet and measured. Considered. Slow.

It helped that I knew that Bruce was a recovering alcoholic and a Vietnam vet. I knew that, like me, he'd seen things that people shouldn't have to see, endured things that people shouldn't have to endure. I didn't know a lot about him, but I knew he understood darkness.

Every week, once a week and sometimes more, I'd go to Bruce's office and scream, rant, rave and bang the sofa. I'd weep and wail for a really long time. Bruce always had tissues and a wastepaper basket out for me. Mostly, he just listened, intently and completely. He never moved to hug me or put a hand on my shoulder. This was a good thing, because, at that time, any physical comfort would've short-circuited my grief. Sometimes, though, when I'd finished crying, I'd look up and see tears standing in his eyes.

Bruce never tried to cheer me up. I'd say, "I'm never gonna be happy again," and he'd say in a neutral voice, "That could be true. It's possible." I'd say, "There's a part of me that's dead and will never come alive again," and he'd respond in that same, matter-of-fact way, "Yeah, that sounds about right. You're not going to be quite alive in the same way ever again." I'd say "Life fucking sucks," and he'd reply, only slightly ironically, "Yep, the Bible's right. Life is a vale of tears."

I'd rage a lot, too. About all kinds of things, large and small, but a special peeve of mine was the sentiment that every thing happens for a reason. No one had the nerve to say that to me about Jesse, but I heard people say it a lot about other stuff. You know the type, people who insist that every storm cloud has a silver lining, the ones who say, cheerily, "Oh, I know you lost your job three months ago, but I bet you'll get one that's even better. You see, everything happens for a reason." Whenever,

I overheard that, I'd silently scream. You idiot. Everything happens for a reason? Really? You want to give me one good fucking reason why my daughter died?

In one session with Bruce, I said through gritted teeth, "The next person who says, 'Everything happens for a reason,' I swear I'll put my fingers around their neck and choke them to death." I illustrated by putting my hands out in front of me and squeezing the life out of the imagined victim. "And you'll have to bail me out of jail." His response came slowly, but I could tell he meant it. "I'd not only bail you out of jail," he said, "I'd defend you on the grounds of justifiable homicide."

The most dramatic session I had with Bruce took place about eight months after Jesse died. My son, Cory, was more torn up by his sister's death than I'd realized. He was away at college and, unbeknownst to me, became involved in some very destructive behaviors One night, I got one of those terrible middle-of-the-night phone calls that every parent dreads. I won't go into the details, but let me just say that for some period of time, I felt strongly that his life was in jeopardy, that I might lose both my children. One day, during the worst of it, I walked into Bruce's office and calmly said, "If Cory dies, I'm going to check out myself." I'd decided that I couldn't endure the death of both my kids. "I'm going to buy a gun," I told him, and then shared the rest of my detailed plan.

Now, it's never fun for a therapist to sit face-to-face with a suicidal client. It's our job to prevent suicide. So Bruce's response was remarkable, one I'll never forget. He didn't call 911; he didn't send me for a psychiatric evaluation; he didn't try to talk me into checking myself into a hospital. He didn't even make me sign of those commitment-to-stay-alive contracts. All he said was "If that happens, and that's what you decide, I'll absolutely understand why. I'll feel sad, But I'll in no way blame you." Basically, Bruce gave me permission to commit suicide. To me it meant that he was meeting me human-to-human, not shrink-to-patient. It meant he understood that perhaps there's some pain in life that people shouldn't be expected to bear. That empathy was precious to me. I had a place to go, week after week, year after year, as long as I needed, where I could sit down and say, "Yup, still feel like dying," and this man would say to me, "Got it. Understood."

It's 12 years later. Cory is doing well. In fact, later this year he'll receive a PhD in philosophy from Princeton. And sometime after Jesse died, I adopted two older girls, sisters, who were growing up in a Guatemalan orphanage. They're my heart, and the three of us continue to heal each other every day.

It's also true that a part of me is dead, and isn't coming back. It's true that my life will never be the same, or as happy as it was when Jesse was alive. Once, I heard a parent say about the enduring effects of losing a child, "It's like the backdrop of my life is painted blue." That's what it's like for me. Still, these days the foreground of my life is pretty damn good. Sometimes, I can even say I'm happy.

In no small measure, I owe that to Bruce.

The world needs more Bruces and it is not necessary that they all be therapists. The act of really listening and walking with another person through their pain is a great gift and a powerful source of healing.

I believe that we all are called to give these gifts to each other, for that is where peace begins.

fifteen

No Big Deal

*Do your little bit of good
where you are:
It's those little pieces of good put together
that overwhelm the world.*
—Desmond Tutu

No Big Deal

Viewing love as a verb makes it easy to understand and relate to the practice of Tikkun Olam, a concept in Jewish mysticism.

Literally, the term means "repair of the world." As I understand it, this "repair" is related to the spread of good deeds throughout the world, whether those deeds are protecting the environment or providing acts of kindness to help others along the way.

In the mystical sense, it has been described as an awareness that there is a storage of God's divine light in the world. That light has been spilled out and spread all over the earth.

So our job on this earth is to collect these pieces of the divine and, through acts of kindness, spread this light throughout the world. This then, will be how peace begins.

These shards of light are always present, if we take the time to recognize them. Sometimes, the healers themselves are not always aware of the enormity of their gift.

This is how I experienced it after my granddaughter, Michelle, was brutally murdered. Michelle's parent's, Pacita and Kevin suffered through a tsunami of pain and grief so great that it could only be grasped by someone else who had also suffered through the tragic death of a child.

The healing hands and hearts and prayers of so many family and friends helped. But, I will always have a special place in my heart for Father Doug of Saint Mary's Catholic church.

He brought his own healing light into Kevin and Pacita's lives. In the three years following Michelle's death, Father Doug met with them week after week, shining a ray of light on their dark path.

Like most of those who spread the light, Father Doug continues to turn aside any mention of gratitude for his gift of caring. So, ultimately, I had to resort to giving him a note so that he know how great was his gift. For my own gratitude reminder, I have kept a copy of that note.

> *Father Doug, because you have so profoundly touched the life of my family, I count you as my friend. When it comes to gratitude, there are not enough words to express the gratitude that I hold in my heart for you.*
>
> *I believe that God touches His people with angel dust and it is those who let it in their hearts who become our angels on this earth.*
>
> *And even though those angels look like everyone else, they shine the light where it is needed. As you have walked with Kevin and Pacita, while they have struggled through their darkest hours, you have been a beacon of that light.*
>
> *Thank you, my angel friend.*

If you view angels as bearers of light, then they are all around us. They are the light that personifies the experience of love as a verb, which echoes all through Judaism and Christianity.

Anne Benefield, the pastor of Geneva Presbyterian Church, spoke to this concept of caring-in-action a Palm Sunday sermon post.

> *Palm Sunday is confusing. It seems so strange to celebrate Jesus' triumphant entry into Jerusalem, knowing what will follow –knowing the coming betrayal and horror. ——How could he not experience anger and irritation?——*
>
> *——I believe that Jesus was drawing strength from the crowds. They were filling His cup. He was taking in this glorious celebration of His arrival.—*
>
> *——Tomorrow would come. During the first part of the week, he would be teaching and healing. He had work to do. There was no time for Him to waste. Today was a day for rejoicing, tomorrow would be A day of work.——*
>
> *——We think of His work as so much different from ours, but the foundation of His work is much like ours. He was reconciling the world to God through his kindness.*

—Reverend Benefield tells of a father, who, when checking on the Geneva Day School for his children, when he stumbled into an adult class.—

—At the end of the class, the father asked if he might return. Later, he took the teacher aside, pointed to the Bible and asked, "What is this book really about?"

The teacher answered, "'kindness.' If you are kind, you will fill all the expectations in this book."

If we want to be faithful to our Lord, we must get in the habit of doing kind things. Make coming up with something kind to do the first thing you think about when you get up in the morning.

Not only will you come up with some wonderful ideas, you will start your day on a positive footing and the rest of the day will follow.

And that, I would add, is because we are the Easter people.

I think that Reverend Benefield would agree, that when we speak of a life of kindness, it is not about all the big show stopping, miracle stuff. It is just those every day little bits of kindness that let the shards of light come into the world.

In Judaism, this is what tikkun olam is all about. Life is made up of all those ordinary, little experiences that somehow turn out to be the shard of light that will make a difference in our lives.

Coffee Two started out as one of those ordinary experiences. It was during the coffee hours between services at Saint Mark Presbyterian Church that I often found myself, like many others, wanting to have less structure and be free to just continue talking together with old friends and welcoming new ones. And that is how Coffee Two, an unofficial extension of coffee hour, came to be.

Responding to a brief notice in the church newsletter, a few people began showing up in the church parlor on Tuesday mornings.

As promised, there was no structure, no Bible study, no prayer and no agenda —just coffee and whatever friends happened to show up, often bearing doughnuts, cookies or fruit.

On one such Tuesday, we met the man from Texas. When I entered the kitchen to fill up the coffee urn, there he sat at the counter, quietly eating the church administrator's lunch.

Under an old, straw cowboy hat, his long, gray hair hung in a scraggly pony tail and his clothes looked as worn and tired as his face. He said that his name was Sam.

"I'm not a bum," said Sam. "I know I look like one, but I've been on the road for several days." As it turned out, the only reason that he was at Saint Mark at all, was because Joe, our building superintendent, happened to be there when Sam came by to ask directions. Joe then kindly took the time to hear Sam's story.

When Susan, the church administrator, stopped by and saw the tired, hungry man, she immediately gave him her lunch, which he was rapidly downing when I arrived.

Sam was a Vietnam vet, living on disability. He had driven to Washington, D.C. with a fellow AA member, for a rally and to see the Vietnam Memorial.

Unfortunately, Sam's "recovering" friend stole Sam's money and went on a bender, taking the car with him. Sam, without food or money, had spent the last two days walking from D.C. to our suburban, Rockville, Maryland neighborhood. He did not want a handout, just a chance to get to the highway so he could thumb a ride back to Texas.

With only a little encouragement, Sam agreed to stay and have coffee with the group. Although, thin to the point of emaciation, Sam never mentioned being hungry. He just waited until the snack platter was passed around. Each time, he gratefully selected another doughnut.

"Please help us finish these," I insisted later, passing the now nearly empty snack plate to Sam. "They'll just go to waste."

As I leaned over Sam, I rested my hand on his back and felt the knobby bones of hunger, while Sam quickly finished off the last two doughnuts.

Sam remained to talk with us and was soon sharing his history. His story was not depressing. It was one of hope and a testament to the human spirit.

He showed us photographs of the abused animals he had rescued, rehabilitated and relocated to new homes. With little in the way of material things, Sam had clearly built a meaningful life, married a woman he loved dearly and became known locally, as the man who saved animals from abuse and neglect.

"No big deal," as Sam told it.

What was a big deal though, was hearing Sam express how, for him, as it has been for so many Vietnam veterans, the wounds of that war still continue to haunt many of the survivors.

Sam's words gave us all a face to the term, "post traumatic stress disorder." His visit to the Vietnam Memorial had stirred up many old feelings and memories, which still brought tears to his eyes.

The memorial is not so far from the Pentagon, where old men plan the wars that young men and women will fight. The memorial honors those vets who never came back, but simply live on as a name on that shiny, black wall.

They are there —all 50,000 names—so that we will never forget what war really means. And they are there so all the Sams, who survived, but were never the same again, can go and touch all that is left.

"I ran my hands over and over all the names," Sam told us. "Finally, I just sat on the ground and cried for hours." Our group had no platitudes of comfort for him. We could only be there in the silence of caring.

Sam asked for nothing but directions to Route 66. Dean and Dorothy, who were active in a support network, decided that just giving directions was not enough. They drove Sam to the InterFaith Works. Hours later, he had a one-way bus ticket to Texas and a ride to the bus station.

To Dean and Dorothy, who spent their entire day assuring that Sam was safely on his way home, this was no big deal. It was just something that needed to be done.

Fortunately, Sam would have enough money to provide food for the two-day bus trip.

"I have a disability check coming in a few days," protested Sam, as some of the group members quietly slipped him some bills. "I can pay you back."

"Just pass it on to the next hungry person," was the whispered response.

"You guys really are Christians, but you're not Bible thumpers," were Sam's parting words. Well, maybe not, unless you think that there is more than one way to thump a Bible.

No big deal. It was just another day at Coffee Two. And yet, a phrase keeps returning to my mind: "Where two or three are gathered in my name......."

No big deal.

sixteen

Growing Up in Eden

*Those who contemplate
the beauty of the earth
find reserves of strength
that will endure as
long as life lasts.*
—Rachel Carson

Growing Up in Eden

The gradual – and not so gradual – breakdown of natural habitat that is endangering the earth's ecosystems is not just threatening plants and wildlife.

We humans are also losing our own peaceful habitat. We just don't recognize it yet. After all, who needs the reality of nature's abundance and natural beauty when "virtual reality" is available?

Technologically advanced communications and recreational opportunities abound. Movies, television, i-pads, computer games and the Internet, which offers every second- hand experience you could imagine; all compete to provide us with a complete audio and visual reality.

Perhaps one day we will be able to see everything –and feel nothing.

The very young enter this world with the gift of wonder for all the earth has to offer. Just watch a young child without any brightly colored Fisher-Price toys to entertain her.

She can play happily for hours in the grass, examining each clump and prying apart the blades to discover an anthill teeming with life; or a whole variety of bugs, each one a new discovery.

Then add some dirt and sticks and maybe a few wooden blocks. Voila! The world of miniature houses, forts and roadways emerges.

The wondering child does not need a steady diet of shiny, colored, educational toys. For the burgeoning creativity of the growing child, the earth *is* an educational toy. If you haven't experienced this world, just join a child. Get on your hands and knees on the ground and they will show you.

Just being aware of beauty is another level of education too often overlooked. Sometimes it is all around us. Mindlessly, we look but we do not see.

A little child will teach you about that. Just watch him examine a flower. With awe, he gazes and then touches the petals, puts his nose into the center – and smiles.

Okay, the flower may get a little mangled in the process. But this is one of nature's worthy sacrifices. For the child's next growth step will be to value and care for things of beauty.

How quickly this awareness can disappear in a world of children's computer games and techno-toys. Soon, organized youth sports enter the scene. The earth now becomes something to run upon on the way to first base. Gradually earth awareness fades as developing skills and "winning," trump "being."

My friend, Margaret, understands this all too well. Of course, this is to be expected. A lover of nature's beauty, Margaret is the one who can be found on a church retreat walking along the shoreline as others swim in the surf.

She is taking in the beauty all around her while she gathers driftwood and leafy branches to display on the altar for the evening service.

Margaret often speaks of another of her joys, visiting her young goddaughter, Catherine, who at six is precocious and charming, possessing the verbal and social gifts of a much older child.

For Margaret, as one who warms to the experience of the divine in nature, these visits are also an opportunity to share the fullness of those experiences with her beloved goddaughter.

During one visit, recounts Margaret, she and Catherine both awakened early in the morning. As was her custom, Margaret went first to the window to look out and see what the day would hold for her.

The sunrise was so beautiful that to this day, Margaret can still recall every detail. Overhead was the soft gray haze of dawn with fluffy blue and purple clouds rolling across the sky in ever shifting patterns. Beyond the drifting clouds, the sun began its ascent with sparkling rays of red and gold shining through the clouds.

Awestruck, Margaret watched in silence for a few moments, until she felt that this was an experience too beautiful not to be shared.

"Catherine," she called, "come and see this gorgeous sunrise!"

"Oh, I see that every day," responded Catherine with a disinterested shrug.

Except that, she really didn't see it at all. For, at six, the world of advanced toys and beginning computer tech, that Catherine, like most of our bright children, inhabits is focused on acquiring ever new data and skills; not on sensory experiences.

So, at six, Catherine has already lost some of early childhood's sense of wonder. It will take someone who still knows that world to re-open those doors for all our Catherines. As for *this* Catherine, I am quite sure that this is going to happen.

For, you see, I know her godmother.

***

It is in the interest of future generations that we have more Margarets now: godmothers, parents, grandparents, and teachers who reawaken our children to the natural world. If Mother Earth is to be preserved it will be by people who love her. Hopefully, we are raising those people now.

Some children just naturally "tune in" to the earth on their own. Of course, it helps if you are one of the lucky ones who lives in a rural area with nature's beauty all around you.

Emily Millen, now a co-ed, was one of those children. Growing up in the West Virginia countryside with parents who were both veterinarians, Emily was blessed to spend her youth surrounded by animals and nature.

Did the young Emily know that she was growing up in Eden? Apparently she did, for at age eleven Emily displayed her own mindful awareness in the following piece:

REFLECTIONS ON AN AUTUMN DAY

The trees overhead make a
great sound of letting down their
dry rain.

The sky beneath the trees
turns wondrous colors of reds,

yellows, browns and oranges,
The entire hillside is blanketed
in a wave of color.

The thunderous roar of the
leaves deafens one who is so
lucky to hear it.

The crunching sounds of
squirrels running around the
bottom of the great oak,
hoping to find a small treasure
enclosed in a nut.

The silence of the golden sun
resting its rays upon the autumn
colors is peaceful.

Little children getting out of a bright
yellow school bus go running out into
the autumn. They rush in and
pounce on the leaves like a cat
after cheese.

What's so spectacular about these
autumn leaves? Is it their ability
to paint the sky? Is it their ability
to sound like the pitter patter of rain?

I will leave it up to you, for it is
all in the eye of the beholder.

-Emily Millen
Age 11

Amen!

***

162 | Alice G. Miller, PhD

Maybe one day Emily will teach her children to love the earth, just as Rob's grandfather taught him. Rob, who works full time at the Truffula Seed Farm in Maryland, grows vegetables, fruits and flowers, which he sells at a nearby road stand. But, Rob's real loves are the hundreds of zinnia plants and acres of sunflowers that he lovingly tends.

As a sort of suburban Johnny Appleseed of flowers, Rob has sown sunflower seeds throughout the roadside patch he occupies. People drive by and smile with pleasure. Others stop to pick to their hearts content.

Inspired by the summers he spent as a boy working on his grandfather's farm, Rob shaped his love of the earth and growing things from the lessons he learned there.

"Now I'm putting something back," says Rob, smiling as he describes the practice he calls "guerilla gardening."

The "guerilla attacks" involve hundreds of sunflower seeds planted randomly in area lots, parking areas and anywhere else they might be enjoyed. He sees this as just the gift of a little random beauty.

However, the greatest gift that Robin shares is the gift of himself. Recently, he has spent time with an elementary school class helping the children to plant a garden.

It is not just the planting that captures the children's interest. It is learning about habitat and the value of birds and toads and insects. They love being a part of planting milkweed for the early stages of butterfly life and buddleia bushes for food, as the adult butterflies mature.

Little children don't read gardening texts. But when a good-looking, warm and friendly young man talks –they listen. And one of those little listeners may just be tomorrow's environmentalist.

How appropriate that Rob's farm should be called the "Truffula Seed Farm," which, he explains, is a whimsical reference to the Dr. Seuss children's book, *The Lorax*.

The Lorax is a little, fuzzy man-creature, who repeatedly declares, "I am the Lorax. I speak for the trees."

All the while, the story continues, the greedy "Once-ler," a stand-in for the environmentally incorrect industrialist, continues to chop down the forest truffula trees in order to create a product called the Threed, "that people don't really need."

At the close of the story, the Once-ler has destroyed the forest for profit. Now only the stumps of the chopped off truffula trees remain. The barren landscape no longer provided habitat and all the living creatures disappeared. This piece of children's fiction is beginning to sound like a preview of our future history.

Alone and bereft, the Once-ler tells the story of his downfall to a visiting young boy. The boy listens, eager and intent. So, hopefully, the Once-ler drops the one last truffula seed into the hand of the young boy.

"Build a new forest," he instructs the boy, "so the living creatures will return at last." You are the hope of the future, the Once-ler tells the boy and insists that he must care a lot.

> *"Or nothings going to get better," he warns.*
> *"It's not."*

So, the moral here is that if we want things to get better, we need to "care a lot" and we need people like Rob, who are planting seeds and flowers and teaching the children about the earth. And, as Rob says:

"If you don't like the way things are going,
plant flowers —not bombs."

seventeen

The Web of Life

*Nature has no
human inhabitant
who appreciates her.*
—Henry David Thoreau

The Web of Life

Thoreau was not totally right when he stated that nature has no human inhabitant who appreciates her. But, he was certainly right about many of the corporations and mining companies who make a business out of exploiting her.

Thoreau would have been appalled had he been there when I received that first call from a Pennsylvania mining company, notifying me that I was one of the heirs to the mineral rights beneath a parcel of oil-rich land. It felt like I was holding the winning ticket to a lottery that I hadn't even entered.

All I had to do, it seemed, was to sign a document agreeing to lease my rights to the mining company and I would be rewarded with an attractive signing bonus, followed by monthly checks, reflecting my share of the profits for the next 20 years.

This was almost too good to be true; getting a lot of money for nothing. But, "nothing" would come with a price, I discovered, after doing a little research. That price would be that I would have to live with myself.

For what the mining company representative had neglected to mention was that this land was in the Marcellus shale region outside of Pittsburgh. Already this area has been subjected to heavy fracking. The monetary gains will be large, but the environmental price will be even larger.

Fracking involves the hydraulic shattering of the shale layer as a means of extracting trapped energy beneath the surface. In this process millions of gallons of water, sand and chemicals are injected at pressure powerful enough to fracture the rock.

The miners can now enter the earth below the aquifer and around the now available oil or gas well. No mining company has ever come up with a plausible explanation for what is to become of the water, which has been contaminated with hundreds of chemicals, some of which are known carcinogens.

That water will remain an environmental threat for generations. Habitats will be destroyed and plant life will suffer. Those who reside in the mined area will now be faced with contaminated water.

I think that since the executives of the mining companies involved in fracking, insist that there is no risk to the water supply, they should be willing to drink the polluted water that they have created. There should be a video of their faces when they are presented with a glass of brown water.

It did not take much research to discover that, all too often, these fracked wells will begin to leak. No surprise there, since the harsh process of fracking has already cracked the shale to free the oil or gas, it can also crack the area around the well.

It does not appear that the mining companies have come up with any solutions for controlling the leaks, which can contain methane gas that will contaminate the atmosphere for years to come. Nor, does it appear that the mining companies consider this to be a matter of any concern.

What is happening in Pennsylvania is happening across the country. Living in the extended Washington, D.C. area, I am aware that this will soon be affecting our space, too. Reportedly, Pennsylvania already has 16,000 miles of streams, polluted with mine drainage and agricultural run-off, which is leaving a path of destruction that will find its way into our own Chesapeake Bay.

The corporations behind the mining are not worried about the Environmental Protection Agency's "suggestions." And that is only going to get worse. The EPA now appears to be losing what few teeth it had.

"Who gets rich and who suffers?" is not a question that any corporation is likely to ask. We have entered an era of increasing corporate greed. This greed mentality overwhelms any morality for the earth or her people.

I am not the sort of hero who tries to save the environment by lying down in front of bulldozers. I don't have that much faith in the drivers' willingness to apply the brakes in time.

So, there was only one way my part in the chance to enjoy the "riches" from this mining "opportunity" could end. I refused to sign the lease to my mineral rights. This was not an easy decision. As several friends have pointed out: "The fracking will continue anyway. You just won't have the money."

This may be true, but I am still able to look in the mirror every morning. And, I am still holding out hope that there will be an increasing number of people who own the mineral rights to oil-rich land and will refuse to lease that land to mining companies. Together, we could all make a difference.

Or, will there just be too many who listen to a leadership that sees only the chance for profit and turns a blind eye to the destruction of our country? I cannot believe that this will become America's new mantra:

"Oh, what the frack....."

What the frack?, indeed. I attempted to post these ideas in an op-ed piece, in spite of the fact that an earlier post accomplished little other than irritating people. My experience with a Pennsylvania paper was most discouraging.

The Pittsburgh-Post Gazette writers sloughed me off to other equally disinterested writers and the editor would not return my phone calls.

The EPA staff in Pennsylvania were very friendly, but unwilling to take any aggressive action to stop the fracking. Instead, they indicated that they would be willing to "monitor" the progress, as the fracking continued.

On a local level, our own city paper expressed little interest in the subject, in spite of the fact that the Chesapeake Bay would ultimately be affected by the run-off from the fracking in Pennsylvania.

I am trying to remain optimistic and believe that the interests of corporate advertisers do not play a role in "encouraging" our newspapers to avoid expressing much concern about the effect of fracking in their local environments.

Many of the people, who have chosen to ignore the threat of fracking, are the same people who believe that the climate crisis does not exist, even with all scientific evidence to the contrary.

For these people, the crisis does not exist, because it has not touched them – yet. Their children and grandchildren will be paying the price.

These are the same people, many of who, are my good friends, but, who laugh at Rob of Truffula Farm, for his simplistic view of the environment. Yet, Rob, who has taught young children about plants and flowers, may also have touched some young people, who will grow up to be the environmentalists who will protect tomorrow's world.

In a less positive way, that is how it happened with me. It was one of my own childhood experiences that forever changed how I would view the world of nature and her inhabitants.

Witnessing the destruction of helpless creatures can instill in a young child, a deep sense of awareness that we all have a responsibility to care for God's creation, before it is too late.

All too well, I know this to be true, because I grew up a long way from Sunny Brook Farm. My father, who had suffered his own painful experiences in childhood, all too often, passed those experiences on to his own children.

Yet, this same angry man found a calming refuge in his garden. Every year, in the early spring, Pop planted hundreds of yellow cosmos seeds. By mid-summer, those cosmos had been weeded, watered and coddled into masses of thick, luxurious plants that burst forth into a golden blaze that lasted for many weeks.

I loved that flowery hillside. It became the inspiration that led me down my own path to becoming a gardener. And, as I watched those flowers prosper, I secretly yearned to be on the receiving end of all the nurture that he lavished on those cosmos.

One summer day, my father smiled as he watched me on the terrace, standing amidst his golden flowers, awestruck by the beautiful butterflies flitting among the blossoms. "Flutter-byes," he called them.

"Would you like to have your own butterfly collection?" asked my father.

"Oh yes," I sighed, delighted by my father's enthusiasm.

But, I had no idea what he had in mind. So I waited in anticipation as Pop disappeared into the house. Soon, he returned, proudly carrying his new creation; a hastily improvised butterfly net made from yards of gauze and several twisted coat hangers.

Then the carnage began. One by one, the beautiful butterflies were snagged into the net, where they floundered, helplessly batting their bright wings against their gauze prison.

When all the struggling had ceased, my father transferred the now still bodies to stiff sheets of white cardboard. I no longer remember how my father actually killed them. I guess I don't want to.

Deftly, he opened and spread the beautiful wings and pinned them flat against the cardboard. The job completed, he now added the finishing touch; a clear sheet of thin plastic, which he taped across the back of the stiff cardboard.

Proudly, my father presented his gift: a silent, dead replica of former beauty, now stilled forever. Mutely, I eyed my present, gulping back the contents of my stomach, which kept threatening to make an appearance.

"Thank you," I mumbled, trying to hide my welling tears, as I pretended to appear grateful for his efforts. But, inside, I just felt tarnished by my lie. Somehow, it felt as though I was responsible for all this destruction.

No more "flutter-bys" flitted past in all their glory. Now, all that remained of their gentle life force was a few cardboard sheets of neatly mounted specimens, in case someone wanted to know how a butterfly had once looked.

That was the day that I became an environmentalist.

***

By now, even the most casual reader is likely to be abundantly aware that I am an unabashed, tree-hugging weenie. Consequently, I feel deeply empowered by Al Gore and his book, *An Inconvenient Truth*.

The reader of *An Inconvenient Truth* is left with the sobering awareness that our world is facing a climate crisis of global proportions. But, we are also left with the desire to see this as a wake-up call, an opportunity to play a role in the reversal of the destruction of the earth.

We have all played a role in this destruction, with our heavy use of pesticides, fossil fuels, energy sources and toxic chemicals; all of which have contributed to the contamination and depletion of our water supply. Not to mention the steady depletion of our trees, green space and wildlife habitat. We have paid a high price in order to make room for more buildings, parking lots and highways.

Goodbye trees. Hello carbon dioxide.

Has everyone forgotten that trees have always been the unsung heroes of the earth? They inhale carbon dioxide and toxins and exhale them as oxygen; a great way to slow global warming. These same trees can also shade a home and reduce energy expenditure for air conditioning.

Every time we plant a tree we contribute to this process. Sadly enough, for every tree we plant we are already losing more to building, lumbering and early death.

When large numbers of trees are randomly chopped down for "development" and "growth," a whole chain of events begins. With the trees gone, the sun begins to dry out and compact the soil that was once beneath them. Plants and understory shrubs that once flourished here now wither and die.

Without the shelter and food that once provided habitat for animals, insects and other living creatures, they, too, disappear. And another piece of the large web of life has been ripped apart. All have been sacrificed for more cars and roads to lead us to more shopping centers, which will further pollute our world.

"We are dumping so much carbon dioxide into the earth's environment that we have literally changed the relationship between the earth and the sun," writes Al Gore.

"So much of that CO2 is being absorbed into the oceans that, if we continue at the current rate, we will increase the saturation of calcium carbonate to the levels that will prevent formation of corals and interfere with the making of shells by sea creatures."

"Global warming, " says Gore, "along with the cutting and burning of forest and other critical habitats, is causing the loss of living species at a level comparable to the extinction event that wiped out the dinosaurs 65 million years ago."

"That event," concluded Gore, "was believed to have been caused by a giant asteroid. This time it is not an asteroid colliding with the earth and wreaking havoc. It is us."

Thinking globally, all the nations of the world need to work together to solve this crisis. As Americans, we need to push our country to become more concerned about the environment, especially at a time when our country's leadership sometimes feels corporate-led than government-led.

Thinking locally, sometimes all you can do is just what little you can. And that usually feels like a drop in the bucket. But, that drop may be an investment for our children and grandchildren.

"Just because you will not see the work completed," the Torah reminds us, "does not mean that you are free not to take it up."

Politically, that may mean voting "green" on issues, whether you are Democrat or Republican. Or, maybe supporting the opposition to constructing one more "inter-county connector," which is just a euphemism for incurring billions of dollars in debt to build yet another highway that will destroy more habitat and add more pollution.

These same highway developers, who question the importance of factoring in the earth's needs, might well think about God's response to Job. And poor Job wasn't even building an inter-county connector.

> *Where were you when I laid the*
> *Foundation of the earth?*
> *Tell me, if you have understanding.*
> *Who determined its measurements—*
> *surely you know!*
> *Or who stretched the line upon it?*
> *Or who laid its cornerstone,*
> *When all the morning stars sang together,*
> *and all the songs of God shouted for joy?*

eighteen

Breathing Room

Don't just do something,
sit there.
—Zen saying

Breathing Room

"Ours is a time of anxiety," Catholic theologian, Thomas Merton wrote more than half a century ago. "Sanctity," said Merton, "means traveling from the area of anxiety to the area in which there is no anxiety...... learning from God, to be without anxiety in the midst of anxiety."

Merton wrote those words without ever experiencing today's massive traffic jams, cell phones, texting, computers, e-mails, instant messaging and multi-tasking. All of which, allow us to remain in constant contact with friends, family, work and all the related problems, which follow us constantly, wherever we go.

Usually, the stresses we all experience are not so much the dramatic, life-threatening fight-or-flight situations of a different era. But rather, they are the steady, unrelenting pressures of daily living in a wired world.

In one of his typically insightful comments, the Dalai Lama has publically shared his assessment of our tension filled culture. Reportedly, when asked what surprised him the most about our humanity today, the Dalai Lama responded:

> *Man, because he sacrifices his health in order to make money. Then he sacrifices money to recuperate his health. And then he is so anxious about the future that he does not enjoy the present; the result being that he does not live in the present or the future.*
>
> *He lives as if he is never going to die, and he dies having never really lived. "*

So, absent a mugger, a stalker, a car accident or a major, life-threatening crisis, with the resulting short term jolt of adrenaline and stress hormones that, in crisis, can empower the flight to safety, or the strength to fight for survival; instead, we experience an ongoing, constant release of hormones like cortisol, that over time can damage our bodies and weaken our immune systems.

The resulting damage can leave us with less resilience to recover from diseases like cancer, immune disorders and increasingly vulnerable to opportunistic infections.

It is time to learn to step back from life's pressures and to take the time to return to a place of peace. In Zen Buddhism the focus is on letting go and learning to separate from the world. If, for even a brief period, we can do this, we can begin to heal and to know peace.

Trust me, the world will keep right on turning, even without our constant worry, planning and input. As the old Zen saying goes:

> *Sit quietly, doing nothing*
> *spring comes and the*
> *grass grows by itself.*

The ultimate in letting go: "sitting Zazen," means, quite literally, "sitting Zen." This is not a meditation as we experience it in the Western world. There is no mantra or object of focus. Instead, the mind moves to a state of complete emptiness.

When you are sitting Zazen you are not connecting with anything external. This is not problem solving time. You are not thinking about your job, your life or yourself. You do not think *period.*

This experience will be a novel concept for those so married to their job that they are unable to spend even a week at the beach without their cell phone. The electronic umbilical cord is never severed. And the stress goes on.....

One day, those who are wound so tightly to their job, may discover that Bertrand Russell was right: "One of the symptoms of an approaching nervous breakdown is the belief that one's work is terribly important."

If this description fits you, consider trying a new experience. Retreat to a quiet, dim, carpeted room and place a comfortable cushion on the floor. Start by just sitting at ease on your cushion.

Let your breath relax and slow. It is not necessary that you begin with an attempt to stop thinking. Instead, just let your thoughts drift in and out of your mind. Ideally, in time, this experience will become less of a conscious effort and more a process of just allowing the body and mind to let go.

For the stressed out body and mind, sitting Zazen is a healing gift. The heart slows down, the central nervous system relaxes and inner tensions are released.

For the dedicated, the faithful practice of sitting Zazen reaches a destination where one day during practice you are just there – with no conscious mind. Total freedom.

Personally, I have opted not to reach the total attainment of this goal. At my stage of enlightenment, it is sufficient to relax and let go of thoughts, while remaining dimly aware that I do, indeed, have a mind.

Perhaps this view reflects my Western thought process, which just has to question, "If you have reached the state of 'no mind,' then how do you make the decision to push the re-start button?"

What I am learning, with the co-operation of my mind, is to sit in silence, completely relaxed and free of external distractions. Breathing slowly and deeply, I am able to clear my thoughts and experience a calming release.

***

For me, the garden becomes an alternative to the Zazen cushion. Just experiencing my leafy, woodland, where the uppermost tree branches overlap and form a thick canopy, which produces an ever changing filter for the sun's rays, allows me to let go and become immersed in the play of light and shadow.

Sometimes, lying in the hammock, lulled by its gentle rocking and the sounds of the birds and squirrels overhead, I can breathe deeply and become at one with the garden world. This, then, is my wordless meditation, which opens the door to spiritual awareness.

In these moments I have come to experience the truth of the words of Teilhard de Chardin, a French Jesuit priest: "We are not human beings having a spiritual experience. We are spiritual beings having a human experience."

Getting to this level of meditation begins with the simple practice of relaxation. For, if your nervous system is in high gear and your body is in a state of tension, your mind is likely to be filled with the chatter of many busy thoughts.

In the world of Zen this state of rambling or racing thoughts is described as the "monkey mind." As long as this "monkey mind" is operating there will be no meditative experience.

Learning to calm your body, and with it, the "monkey mind," is the start of relaxation. Beginning a practice of learned relaxation starts with the awareness of tension that you are already holding and then progresses to consciously releasing that tension.

STEPS TO RELAXATION

1. Lie on a comfortable, flat surface. With your arms loosely at your sides, stretch until all parts of your body feel aligned and evenly supported. Close your eyes and gently inhale through your nose. Breathe deeply through your chest and into your belly. Shallow breathing that stops at your chest does not allow the extra oxygen to enter deeply into your body and provide extra relaxation. Then slowly exhale through your mouth and allow the air to gently exit your body.

2. Turn your attention to your legs. Tighten your thighs, your buttocks, your knees and your calves. Press your heels into the floor. Feel the tension mount as you hold those muscles as tightly as possible.

Then make a conscious decision to release them. Do it slowly and feel the change as your muscles begin to relax. Take several deep slow breaths and experience the relief. Be aware of the difference when you feel the relaxation. In time, your body will learn to recreate this.

3. Now move your focus to your abdomen, your stomach and your chest. Simultaneously, clench the muscles in all these areas. Hold that action and feel the burn as your tired muscles ache for relief.

Again, consciously decide to slowly release those muscles. Inhale and exhale for several slow breaths. Feel the relief as your stressed muscles now ease into relaxation.

4. Once again prepare to tense up. This time tighten and lift your shoulders into the stress position. Clench your jaws, squeeze your eyes shut and press the back of your head into the floor.

178 | Alice G. Miller, PhD

As you maintain this position be aware of the increasing discomfort and stress. Now make a choice to let that tension slowly leave your body. Feel how good it is to be aware of all that stress.

Breathe deeply and maintain your awareness of the difference between stress and relaxation. With practice, you will soon be able to recall and re- create this state of physical relaxation, without first going into the stress mode.

5. Allow your breathing to slow and deepen. Feel your body, relaxed and loose, as you lay there, weightless and at peace.

6. In this relaxed state, shift your mind to your breathing. With your eyes remaining shut, place your palms flat on your chest, just over your rib cage.

Now breathe deeply. Feel your hands raise with each inhalation and fall with each exhalation. Remember to let the breath go down into your belly. Experience the *slow, deep* rhythm of your breathing.

7. To maximize your breathing experience, try to leisurely hold your breath following each inhalation. Imagine that you are savoring the fresh air in your newly expanded lungs.

This should be slow and relaxing, not stressful. Know that you are providing life-giving oxygen to your body. Your heart rate is probably slowing and your muscles are relaxing even more fully.

When you are completely comfortable begin to slowly release the breath, taking twice as long to exhale as you did to inhale. Feel yourself letting go of the old, stale, toxin-laden air in your lungs and replacing it with fresh clean air.

Now just lie still and continue to relax. Breathe deeply and enjoy this new feeling.

It is called peace.

***

Being calm in your heart leaves a lot less room there for anger and a lot more room for tolerance. It becomes a pathway for peace.

And that is the pathway that I am choosing. Although, I am still en route, I will know that I am firmly on the path when I can translate my experience of the peace of meditation into the action of a life lived by the words of Reinhold Niebuhr's prayer of serenity:

SERENITY PRAYER

God grant me the serenity,
to accept the things I cannot change.....
Courage to change the things I can,
and the wisdom to know the difference.
Living one day at a time,
Accepting hardships as a pathway to peace.
Taking as He did, this sinful world as it is,
Not as I would have it.
Trusting that you will make all things right
If I surrender to His will.
That I may be reasonably happy in this life,
And supremely happy with Him in the next.

nineteen

Waging Peace

When the power of love
overcomes the love of power,
the world will know peace.
—Jimi Hendrix

Waging Peace

Wherever there are tyrants and terrorists who seek power there will be no peace. Wherever there are angry, unhappy people, who feel that they are being treated unfairly, there will be unrest and uproar. For without justice there can be no peace.

In the seething cauldron that is the Middle East, Jews and Muslims are pitted against each other, as are Muslims against Muslims. And daily they continue to demonstrate that bombs and guns will never provide a solution.

Now, as terrorism threatens the world, there is a rising sentiment in America that we will need to quell the violence with more violence. It struck fear in my heart when I heard the plans for retribution that were suggested by some of the 2016 Presidential candidates.

The promise of former Presidential contender, Ted Cruz, makes one wonder if this is the new face of America that we choose to show to the world:

"We will carpet bomb them into oblivion," said Cruz. "I don't know if sand can glow in the dark, but we're going to find out."

I am afraid that if he were to have become President, what Ted Cruz might have found out is that the result of his campaign promise might well be the start of World War III.

Perhaps, if another war was the goal of Ted Cruz, he would have done well to consider heeding the words of General Eisenhower, a major force behind the American victories in World War II:

> "I hate war as only a soldier who has lived through it can;
> only as one who has seen its brutality, its futility, its stupidity."

Sadly enough, I have no answers; only questions, doubts and a few hopes. In hoping, I can only return to the words of Reverend Martin Luther King: "Hate cannot drive out hate; only love can do that." Operationalizing that belief is a little more difficult.

It is hard to feel much love for people who are entering public places with assault rifles and mowing down droves of helpless victims.

Some of these terrorists, who call themselves religious martyrs, bear a strong resemblance to the classic psychopath, who can, at times, appear to be quite normal. But, the reality is that the psychopath does not comprehend the concept of right or wrong; nor does he possess any shred of empathy or feeling for others.

Love is something that the psychopath neither feels nor accepts. These traits, combined with fearlessness and a lust for excitement, are a recipe for disaster. I call myself a Christian, but when I view the human wreckage caused by their actions, I am unable to feel any love for these predators.

There are others, who appear not to possess the capacity for caring, but whose psychological make-up has made them vulnerable to directions from the hard-core psychopaths. Theorists have speculated that this may have been the behavioral dynamic between the two teenage killers in the 1994 shootings at Columbine High School. I don't believe that the alleged "bullying" these two experienced is sufficient explanation or justification for the violent carnage they avenged on their classmates. But then, who could have predicted or prevented it?

The seemingly weaker of those two boys, was a different sort of victim, as were the parents who loved him. It appeared that he was the willing pawn of his stronger partner. But no one really knows if that is true. No one will ever know how this came to happen. And, by not knowing, we are continuing to see repeated tragedies.

***

Today we face a sad product of all these seemingly random, violent acts of terrorism throughout the world. The mass of refugees, most of whom are victims themselves, are attempting to escape the escalating violence in their own countries.

Because of the terror caused by some of their countrymen, these refugees are now being viewed with suspicion. How, ask their host countries, can we distinguish victims from potential terrorists?

This fear has spread to our own country. Too many Muslim Americans are now viewed as potential terrorists. Historic evidence has indicated that citizens of the Muslim faith have shown no more tendency toward crime than any other faith group.

Assuming that most American Muslims are potential terrorists makes about as much sense as assuming that most Americans, who call themselves Christians, belong to the Ku Klux Klan. Sadly, of course, there are some who do.

When Donald Trump, as a candidate in the Presidential election of 2016, suggested the curtailing of all future Muslim immigration as well as the deportation of American Muslims, he decried all the values that have made America great.

These American Muslims are citizens, who are entitled to the same freedoms as any other citizen. We are all in serious danger of losing those very freedoms if an American President can decide to which citizen the Constitution applies.

It is living by our Constitution that has made America great. How ironical that a contender for the Presidency of the United States would advocate a departure from that Constitution, while simultaneously vowing that HE will make America great.

The writer, Viet Thanh Nguyen, who refers to himself as "once an immigrant and refugee," counters Donald Trump with his own belief: "My America opens its arms to the world, rather than sells the world its arms."

As Christians, we believe in welcoming the stranger. This is who I want to be. But sometimes, like when there is another terrorist attack, I begin wondering about the frightening differences in today's world from the world of Biblical times.

The Bible did not mention welcoming the stranger when that welcome could include the possible infiltration of terrorists, who, themselves, might cause the death of hundreds of innocent victims, who did not deserve to die.

The only answer appears to be that we must find a way to screen out the potential terrorists from those victims who are fleeing oppression.

Finding Peace In Our Thyme | 185

One Face Book poster, who chose to remain anonymous, added a little humor to his suggested solution for solving the problem of potential terrorists entering the country:

> *The Israelis are developing an airport security device that elimi-nates the privacy concerns that come with full- body scanners. It's an armored booth you step into that will not x-ray you, but will detonate any explosive device you may have on your person.*
>
> *Israel sees this as a win-win situation for everyone, with none of this crap about racial profiling. It will also eliminate the cost of long and expensive trials. You're in the airport terminal and you hear a muffled explosion.*
>
> *Shortly thereafter, an announcement: "Attention to all standby passengers, El Al is pleased to announce a seat available on flight 670 to London. Shalom!"*

Yet, it is the Jews, who suffered so much during the Holocaust, who refuse to play the hate game. The Washington, D.C. congregation of Temple Rodef Shalom has welcomed the Syrian refugees. Their Rabbi, Jeffery Saxe, stated in the Washington Post:

> *We as a congregation feel it's especially important for us. Especially as Jews. We're commanded in the Torah to be kind to the stranger, because we were strangers in the land of Egypt. We want to give them a message of welcome, which is not always what they're hearing in this country.*

I believe that is all goes back to finding a way to re-build a world where we are all truly brothers and sisters. Except, I have yet to develop a master plan to accomplish this.

It is inspiring to remember an experience that happened before terrorism reached such global proportions, when a group of Catholic and Protestant Christians found a way to accomplish a peaceful resolu-tion on a much smaller scale.

For years in Northern Ireland, separation and turmoil among Christians had escalated into violence between the Catholics and the Protestants. In America, we Christians like to speak disparagingly

186 | Alice G. Miller, PhD

about the squabbles in other parts of the world, but we ourselves have not exactly emerged with spotless records.

Some years ago a group of American Presbyterian leaders discovered that much of the money used to provide ammunition for the violent uprisings in Northern Ireland was coming from the United States.

Concerned, but misguided, American Protestants and Roman Catholics were quietly bankrolling both sides of the sectarian violence. Most of that money was used for the purchase of weapons.

In a monumental decision, the church leaders concluded that since waging war had never worked, waging peace just might. And that is exactly what happened in Northern Ireland. Peace works.

Just ask Reverend James Macdonell, chair of the Presbyterian Committee for Northern Ireland. Pastor Emeritus of Saint Mark Presbyterian Church, Jim like so many creative people, re-invented himself upon retirement.

People who are moved by issues of social concern and justice will always find a role in this world. Soon enough, Jim found himself moved by the ideas expressed in the oft-repeated words of John Ferguson, a member of the Corryneela Center Community in Belfast, Ireland.

As long as there's injustice
in any of God's Lands,
I am my brother's keeper.
I dare not wash my hands.

So it is not surprising that Jim was soon an active participant in the Presbyterian Community for Northern Ireland, which helped to create an interchurch committee.

Joining together were the American Presbyterian leaders and leaders of the U.S. Conference of Roman Catholic bishops and the Irish Church leaders. No longer a part of the problem, they were all together becoming a part of the solution.

This became quite apparent when, after a number of successful reconciliation meetings, the leaders discussed the possibility of limiting the duration of the meetings.

"Oh no! Please don't leave," their Irish counterparts insisted. "This is the only chance we get to talk with each other."

By word and deed, the interfaith team of two countries and two religious groups began spreading the message, "We are together….." and in doing so, they became a force for healing in Northern Ireland.

Those times became the first stirring of peace. And it all happened because a group of people sat down to talk. They have sent a powerful message to American supporters —both Catholic and Protestant: "Don't send guns. Words are more effective.

Treating each other in a way that says they are respected and valued actually works —sometimes. It worked in Ireland and became one small step toward making the world a better place.

So, if you are truly a dreamer, it means being on the road to the fulfillment of the prophet Isaiah's vision of the Peaceable Kingdom:

> *The wolf shall dwell with the lamb,*
> *and the Leopard shall lie down with the kid,*
> *and the calf and the Lion and the fatling together,*
> *and a little child shall lead them.*
>
> *The cow and the bear shall feed:*
> *their young shall lie together;*
> *and the lion shall eat straw like the ox.*
>
> *The suckling child shall play over the hole*
> *of the asp;*
> *and the weaned infant shall put his hand*
> *on the cockatrice den.*
>
> *They shall not hurt or destroy*
> *in all my holy mountain,*
> *the earth shall be full of the*
> *knowledge of the Lord*
> *as the waters cover the sea.*
> > *—Isaiah 11: 6 – 9*

Would that it were so. But, to quote the revised version of Isaiah, as repeated to me by one of my more cynical friends:

".....the lion may lie down with the lamb," goes the revised version, "but the lamb won't get much sleep."

Probably not. Symbolically though, it is still a worthy goal, at least between humans. But, for thousands of years, mankind has continued to resolve angers and resentments with violence.

The crisis in the Middle East is not a new story. The only evolution in communication appears to have been the upgrade from fists and stones to guns, assault rifles and bombs. We just can't seem to get the concept of burying the hatchet – but not in each other.

***

You don't have to travel to the Middle East to witness this phenomenon. A mini version of the struggles between warring nations can be seen played out every day in our communities, between individuals who cannot handle their own smoldering resentments.

One of my psychiatrist acquaintances had witnessed this phenomenon, all too frequently, in his own therapy practice. He described arriving late one day for a group therapy session with several teenage substance abusers.

As the boys filed into the doctor's office, one boy remained lying on the couch in the waiting room.

"Why don't you come in, too, Bill?" asked the doctor.

"Uh-h, I can't," mumbled the boy, turning his face away.

"Why not?"

"Because," replied Bill, "I think my nose is broken."

Sure enough it was. While waiting for the arrival of a nearby doctor from the same medical building, the psychiatrist laid Bill on the floor and conducted the first part of the group therapy around him.

The group discussed the whole episode quite frankly. Alan, the boy who had hit Bill, admitted that he had been out of control at the time.

"But why did you have to hit Bill?" questioned the doctor.

"I've been mad at him for weeks." admitted Alan.

"Yeah, yeah," seconded the group members.

"If you were mad at Bill, why in the hell didn't you tell him, then?" asked the doctor.

"Ah, well," shrugged Alan, "I didn't want to hurt his feelings."

"So," concluded the doctor, "he broke his nose instead. The boy didn't just have a drug problem. He also had a communication problem."

No peaceable kingdom here. Between individuals as well as between nations, unresolved issues can fester and erupt into violence.

If only Alan, who was sorely lacking in communication skills, had, God forbid, considered talking with Bill a few weeks earlier. But instead, Bill ended up with a crooked nose and Alan's parents ended up fearing a lawsuit, while Alan remained in detention.

Holding onto anger and resentful feelings, as Thich Nhat Hanh reminds us, can eat you up alive. It is, he suggests, like taking poison and waiting for the other person to die.

***

Communication is not always the sole issue. Sometimes in life we just need to know when to simply let it go. In Mother Teresa's words, "If we have no peace, it is because we have forgotten that we belong to each other."

This philosophy is one of the many gifts that Reverend Roy Howard has brought as the Pastor of Saint Mark Presbyterian Church.

"You are God's beloved," he reminds the congregation. "How then can you not value yourself?"

For me, this is where peace comes in. Because, so also is your neighbor the beloved of God. When you really believe this, there is a softening of the boundaries between "us" and "them."

The true peacemakers are the ones who can see "us" and erase "them." Whenever I find myself forgetting this, I have to return to the comfort of the prayer of Saint Francis:

190 | Alice G. Miller, PhD

Prayer of Saint Francis

Lord, Make me an instrument of they peace;
Where there is hatred, let me sow love;
Where there is injury, pardon;
Where there is despair, faith;
Where there is darkness, light;
And where there is sadness, joy.

O Divine Master,
Grant that I may not so much seek
To be consoled, as to console;
To be understood, as to understand;
To be loved, as to love;
For it is in the giving that we receive,
It is in the pardoning that we are pardoned,
And it is in dying that we are born
to eternal life.

Being an instrument of peace, as Reverend Roy Howard has demonstrated, is not always in the big dramatic actions. Sometimes it is just "a story about two men, from vastly different backgrounds, becoming neighbors and building a neighborhood, one fence at a time."

In his own words, this is Roy's story.

This is a story of hope. It's also a story of strangers becoming neighbors. Marduk is my neighbor. We share a fence. "In my country" or "in my village" is how he begins many sentences, having lived in Iran until seven years ago when he moved to Maryland with his wife and two children.

Marduk drives a bus. He leaves for work at 4:00 a.m. He speaks like many others who have learned English on their own. For instance, subject and verb occasionally disagree and words are sometimes left out. "I like, I like," is one of his favorite phrases. When I asked how he learned English, he explained that after the revolution, English was no longer taught in any schools and rarely spoken. (The revolution is code for the fall of the Shah of Iran and the subsequent reign of Iranian fundamentalist and political allies.)

Finding Peace In Our Thyme | 191

I listened to Marduk with curiosity. Once I asked him about his home in the south of Iran. "In my village it is always hot, very hot. Makes Florida seem frigid in the summer." His comment came at the end of a very hot day and the joyous completion of a project I didn't think was possible. I'll explain.

Early in the summer I began negotiations with a contractor to rebuild the twenty-year old sagging wood fence that we share. The price came in much too high. Marduk said, "Let's do it together! We can. We can." I hemmed and hawed, unsure of this budding construction partnership. But my wife agreed.

"That's a great idea. You can do it." When she said that, I sighed, knowing that I was defeated, bracing for the heat and humidity, and knowing how "easy projects" are rarely easy.

Marduk (the name is the same as the ancient Babylonian god) suggested that we go to Lowe's and pick up the fence posts. It is a good experience, culturally and personally to shop at Lowe's with an Iranian immigrant who speaks English with his very distinct grammar. But we did it and to my growing surprise I began to relish the opportunity to work together. Christian and Muslim.

But, I didn't relish it on the day I discovered my tools locked in Marduk's garage when I wanted to work alone on the project. I bounded over to his house. "Why are my tools locked up?" I asked impatiently. He smiled impishly. "We will work together! Not alone. I like us to work together." What could I say to my neighbor taking such happiness in working together? "Okay."

Now the project is done. Marduk stands on his deck and I on mine, admiring our work. "I like, I like," he says, "We do it together!"

And so they did. Marduk did not become one of "them." He and Roy became "us." Once again, this is where peace begins – embracing our neighbor –a concept described long ago in an old Hasidic lesson:

The rabbi asked his students: "How can we determine the hour of dawn, when the night ends and the day begins?"

One of the students suggested: When from a distance you can distinguish between a dog and a sheep?"

"No," was the answer of the rabbi.

"Is it when you can distinguish between the fig tree and the grapevine?" asked the second student.

"No," the rabbi said.

"Please tell us the answer then," said the students.

"It is, then," said the wise teacher, "when you can look into the face of another human being and you have enough light in you to recognize your brother or your sister.

Until then it is night and the darkness is still with us."

twenty

The Voice of the Turtle Dove

*I alone cannot change
the world, but I can cast
a stone across the water to
create many ripples.*
—Mother Teresa

The Voice of the Turtle Dove

My pilgrimage is continuing to evolve and I am finding myself in the process of becoming a more peaceful person.

For me, to be a peacemaker is to be one of those people who Albert Schweitzer calls the "children of the light." And that is who I want to be: a child of the light.

I am still working on that. And in the process I have come to believe that life's search is less about finding out what it is that I am meant to *do*, and more about discovering who it is that I am meant to *be*.

In the process of evolving into who I was meant to *be*, I believe that the answer to the question of what I am meant to *do* simply emerges on its own, as the product of who I am now becoming.

I can't by myself bring peace to the world. But I can experience it, love it and pass it on from time to time. And that, for me, is enough.

Always, I feel a great debt of gratitude to all the people who have loved me and showed me a better way to live.

Like love, this is not a debt to be paid back. It is a gift to be passed on. And that is exactly what I mean to do, with a little help from my friends and my garden.

For it is in the garden that my own spiritual energy is renewed each day. You can't give to others what you yourself are lacking.

When I need to restore my bounce all it takes is half an hour; walking through the woodland, or lying in my hammock listening to the birds and feeling gratitude. Or renewal, for me, sometimes can mean just sitting in the dappled sunlight on my big stone rock beside the pond. And there, I am once again brought back to a place of peace within my world.

This, then, is my peaceable Eden.

***

Everyone needs a place in their life where they can just be still and meditate. For some, it may be a quiet and beautiful room. Or, for others, it may be a long, sandy beach or the still waters of a mountain lake.

But, if you long to have a green and peaceful Eden, you may find great joy in creating one for yourself. Don't let yourself be intimidated by lack of experience. It is far easier than you may think. And nature is very forgiving.

Here is the very first lesson for new gardeners: Forget the old "I don't have a green thumb" excuse. Most of us aren't born with green thumbs. We grow them with use.

Much of what I know about gardening I learned by doing it the wrong way first. So, if you are a beginner, let me save you some time. Here is a simple, foolproof plan for a small meditation spot.

Just start with a small sunny corner in your back yard. Think triangle. Plant a small flowering tree, maybe a dogwood, in the apex of the triangle.

Add three sturdy azaleas in a semi-circle beneath the tree. Space them with ample room for growth and spread. Hint: Delaware Valley white azaleas are very hardy and will tolerate occasional neglect once they are established. The azalea at the center of the semi-circle should be centered a couple of feet in front of the tree's root ball. Scatter in some wildflowers. Voila! You now have a small sanctuary.

Now add a birdbath in front of the middle azalea, sheltered by the tree branches. The branches will provide safe perching spots for the birds. Then add a bird feeder and maybe some sheltering undergrowth around the birdbath area. The wildflowers will do nicely. Congratulations! A mini habitat has begun. You are starting to become a steward of the earth.

With the addition of a curved stone bench, angled to face the birdbath, you have just created a special place to meditate. Leave the stresses of everyday life behind and enter that experience called the "sacred pause."

WARNING: Gardens frequently become addictive. Soon you may want to nurture more shrubs and flowers and provide habitat for more small creatures. When this happens, you start to feel a thrilling and powerful connection to the planet.

Soon, you find yourself beginning to embrace the earth. And then, God forbid, you might become a radical who tries to slow down the destruction of the earth and to nurture and protect what still remains.

That is the way it worked for me. First there was a beginner's garden. Then gradually, I fell in love with more and more trees, shrubs and plants, and the habitats they created.

Eventually, like many other gardeners before me, I became the crazed fanatic that I now am, wanting to share with everyone the wonders of my little piece of the earth. The story of the creation of the garden that has become my peaceable Eden has already been told in *For Everything There is a Season.*

The essence of this garden is captured on an old wooden sign, which hangs over the archway into the garden and prepares the new visitors to be aware that they are entering a place of sanctuary.

"The Thin Place" is the greeting carved into the old wood. And, if you know the Celtic origins of those words, that pretty much says it all.

The early Celtic people believed that in the world of nature there are many "thin places." These are the spots where the membrane between heaven and earth is extremely thin. Here, the Celtic people believed, are the places where man is most closely connected with God. Here is where you will be touched by God.

And here is where I find peace.

***

How fitting it is that the "thin place," that is my garden, is also home to a family of angels. They nestle in the shrubbery, stand tall along the path, sit upon the rocks, hide from sight at the end of a path and recline in the birdbath. All in all, they have made themselves quite at home.

Perhaps my penchant for angels stems back to the years when I was the lone Protestant in Sister Ellen Marie's second-grade class. Poor

Sister never quite adjusted to bearing the cross of having one little seven-year old Protestant defiling her classroom.

Life was hard for both of us. That was the year I first knew what "us" and "them" meant. How could I not? I was "them."

In the name of peace, I shall try to be more forgiving and stop referring to Sister Ellen Marie as my nemesis. If I were a bigger person, I might want to consider that perhaps she may well have had some painful memories of her own that colored her thinking.

If there was one thing that Sister Ellen Marie did believe in, besides rules, it was her angels. The only soft side I ever saw of Sister was those angels.

Always, she was convinced that those angels were watching over her. And you can just bet that none of those angels were former Protestants.

Because Sister was far from being an abstract thinker, I sometimes had difficulty understanding her concrete presentation of *absolute* facts that were NOT to be discussed or questioned.

As a new second-grader, my first assignment was to remember that I must always be sure to sit in exactly one half of my desk seat. The other half of the seat, explained Sister, was for my guardian angel. Well, at least she was willing to share an angel.

"How did my angel get to be an angel?" I wanted to know.

The only answer I ever got was a version of "Yours is not to question why, yours is but to do or……..sit up straight, keep your mouth shut and print nicely." Apparently, the angels valued nice printing.

So, lacking any additional information about angels, I named mine "Angela." Now that is a pretty good name for an angel.

Occasionally, when Sister Ellen Marie wasn't looking, I would give Angela a good poke just to see what she would do. But Angela never responded. Once, I even slid over on Angela's side of the seat. Nothing happened.

Sadly, I wondered if Angela had just left when she, too, found out that I was a Protestant. Fortunately, I knew better than to share that thought with Sister Ellen Marie, who had already pulled my ear for earlier transgressions.

The angel statues that grace my current garden are considerably more concrete than Angela ever was. Well actually, they *are* concrete.

But I always refer to them as stone. Somehow, stone seems more solid and authentic. However, this not being the Garden of Versailles, with a corresponding budget, stone has never been an option.

Amazingly though, with several treatments of yogurt, mud and beer, the statues begin to look quite aged and authentic. The angels know, of course. But they aren't talking.

Occasionally, Stan, my husband, will become a bit testy at the sight of his Michelob being poured gently over an angel. So this is a project better handled in private.

My angels are very important to me and so I treat them with great care. This is why Stan, with his usual kindness and generosity, recently gifted me with a beautiful life-size angel, knowing all the while the amount of Michelob that this was going to cost him.

Radiant with the patina of induced age, my angel graces the entry path in all her glory. And I smile every time I pass her. This angel, like all the others, represents all those qualities inherent in the presence of a guardian angel. They are symbols of being "the beloved," and the one who is watched over.

In life, I believe that we are called to watch over each other and sometimes to be an angel for each other. Certainly, in my own life there have been many people who have been an angel to me.

"So go ahead and laugh," I would say to the occasional cynic who crosses my path. "But, as for me and Sister Ellen Marie, we believe."

***

Now, in remembering how much Sister Ellen Marie's angels meant to her and how badly she seemed to need them, I find myself inching toward tolerance.

Like Sister, I too, have done my share of putting people in boxes. I can well recall one incident; being in the midst of what felt like an important service to someone, while simultaneously considering the possibility of rejecting that person.

It had been one of those moments in life when everything seems to be going so smoothly and then suddenly it all falls apart.

The whole experience started as a very noble project. As church youth advisors, Stan and I wanted to support the kids and their dream of opening their own coffee house, a place where youth of the community would always be welcome.

We participated in the dream; Stan and me and Jim, the Pastor. Although it was always called "The Coffee House," few people actually drank the coffee.

Instead, everyone ate pizza, listened to loud bands, danced and generally had a wonderful time. We had a great time, too. It seemed okay to gloat, just a little. We had all made a dream come true. Then came the crash.

Suddenly and without warning the whole thing blew up. One moment it was a peaceful, swinging coffee house and twenty seconds later we had one split lip and fists flying in all directions.

It all started when Ralph arrived at the coffee house roaring drunk and was refused admittance by Larry, our Keeper- of-the-Door.

"Outta the way, punk!" Ralph snarled, pushing his heavy six-foot frame through the door. But he was momentarily blocked by five feet and five inches of sheer determination and guts.

"You're not coming in tonight, buddy," stated Larry. "You're bombed. Come back next week when you're sober."

Thom, the unofficial coffee house bouncer, leapt to the defense of Larry. Ralph, now enraged, slammed Larry against the wall and muscled his way into the building. But he was no match for Thom and Larry together. As a team, they shoveled the still-protesting troublemaker out the door.

It might have ended there but for the untimely arrival of Sam. Sober, Sam could be the epitome of warmth and friendliness, but when drunk or provoked, he was 230 pounds of pure hell on wheels.

"Get your damn hands off my friend, you dirty bastards," he bellowed, lumbering into the fracas. One swing of Sam's massive fist and Larry's mouth was a bloody mess.

He had picked on the wrong guy. Larry, a member of the high school wrestling team, was a 105 pounds of wiry strength. Suddenly a crowd began to build up and there were murmured threats of retaliation.

That was enough of that. I quietly headed for the phone and asked the police if we might have a little assistance. And ninety- per- cent of the coffee house crowd heard only the loud, throbbing beat of a local band and blissfully unaware, they danced on.

Stan waded into the flailing mass of swinging arms and took Sam firmly by the elbow.

"Now get out of here and get out fast," he said firmly.

"You leave me alone," blustered Sam, ripping his arm free. "Just get your damn hands off me. I don't have to do anything I don't wanna do."

"You'd better leave, Sam," repeated Stan. "The police are on their way."

"I'm never coming here again. This goddamn church is just like the rest of them," Sam roared. "And I'm not afraid of any cop." But he was already retreating at the mention of the magic word "police."

As Sam loped off into the woods muttering choice aphorisms, the police, in their usual unobtrusive manner, slipped in with their red lights flashing and sirens wailing.

Later that night, as the advisors worked with the kids over the cleanup, the air was rancid with bitterness and resentment. I found my "deep" concerns for Sam's wellbeing rapidly evaporating as I pondered how best to eliminate him from the coffee house scene.

"Well," Jim commented disgustedly, "I hope this doesn't blow the whole bit.'

"Yeah," Stan muttered, "what a bunch of winners! A few wise guys spoil it for everybody."

Reflecting on our obvious concern, Thom turned to the Pastor and said, "Gee, Rev, most of the kids had a great time and didn't give us any trouble."

One of the kids interjected, "What are we going to do about the trouble makers? Are you just going to let them get away with it?"

"When I think about Larry's mangled lip," Stan responded.

"I think there is a least one guy we're going to have to deal with personally." Charity and forgiveness were in short supply that night.

The ministry of the coffee house was at a turning point. We had had our first preview of the problems and pitfalls that were yet to come. Now, with the future looking a little dim, the price seemed higher.

"Hey, you guys! Don't let yourselves get all up tight, laughed Tim with a characteristic shrug. "Let's not lose our cool. After all, it might get worse.""

Two days later, with my cool only partially restored, I found myself pacing the sidewalk in front of Sam's house. For thirty-six hours I had delayed this visit, not wanting to approach this unpleasant, but necessary, task in anger.

I rang the doorbell and asked to see Sam alone.

"I know why you're here," said Sam when he came outside. "I know I've been blackballed at the coffee house.

"Don't worry. I'm not coming back." His face reflected despair, not anger.

My well-rehearsed speech dissolved in the face of his straightforward contrition. To my own surprise, I replied without pause.

"We'd like to have you back. The coffee house is for you, too."

Sam looked at me with suspicion, giving hint to his lack of familiarity with acceptance. Slowly then, he began to unfold the weight of his problems. Having recently dropped out of high school, Sam had few social contacts and few places to go.

Most of his time was spent working as a stock boy in a local shopping center. He was lonely and he had almost forgotten that old, unrequited yearning to belong.

I was beginning to realize that the removal of the coffee house from Sam's life would have felt like a final door being slammed shut. Looking back, I am reminded of the words written by Norwegian writer, Arne Gargorg, nearly a hundred years ago:

To love someone is to learn
the song in their heart
and sing it to them
when they have forgotten it.

Sometimes, people like Sam don't even realize that they ever had a song. So now it was time for the coffee house community to sing along with him.

Although he didn't know it yet, Sam's return was also going to involve some therapy and some anger management work.

"But what about Larry?" asked Sam, still doubtful.

"Well, Sam," I replied, "Larry will have to speak for himself." Of course, I already knew how Larry would respond.

The next day after school, Larry invited Sam to return to the coffee house. It came as no surprise when years later, Larry became a minister.

Sometimes out of crisis situations come unlikely endings. We saw proof of this several weeks later when Sam, now a coffee house regular, assumed the responsibility of helping to patrol the coffee house parking lot.

As Sam trudged through the parking lot, effortlessly carrying a huge log on his shoulder, he shouted a warning to his former alcoholic companions.

"Any guys I catch here with booze are really gonna get smashed."

Those were not the words I would have chosen for the church parking lot. But Sam had chosen to remain sober and now he was substituting bluster for brawl.

As we watched him sternly patrolling the lot, the staff laughed hilariously, not *at* him, but *with* him. For Sam was one of us now.

And, once again, this is how peace begins.....becoming "us."

***

Meanwhile, world peace continues to elude me. I just keep on doing the "little stuff" and experiencing deep gratitude for all those people who are doing the "big stuff."

So that maybe –just maybe, someday we really will build a lasting, peaceable kingdom. And then, like the "Song of Solomon," our song for the world will be heard throughout the land.

> *For lo, the winter is past,*
> *the rain is over and gone;*
> *the flowers appear on the earth;*
> *the time of the singing of birds*
> *is come, and the voice of the*
> *turtle dove is heard in our land....*

Let it be so.

Made in the USA
Middletown, DE
14 August 2017